HOW TO STEAL THE CROWN JEWELS

HOW TO STEAL THE CROWN JEWELS

by

Nicholas Green

1stBook – rev. 7/10/00

About the Book

They said it couldn't be done, but it was. The Crown Jewels of Britain were guarded by the best defenses in the world, they were impregnable. Until Captain Rod Jackson, Royal Marine Commandos, saw the way to do it. The vault builders had thought of every possible defense, except one. And it was the British government which unwittingly provided the way in.

In exciting action scenes in Britain and abroad see how the Crown Jewels were stolen, and how the raiding team got away with it. See too the controversial results, and how the course of history was altered. The unexpected twist in the ending will keep you enjoying this book right up to the last page. Completely authentic in its settings and details, the author writes from inside knowledge of the places and people mentioned. The book rings excitingly true because it all happened, in HOW TO STEAL THE CROWN JEWELS.

Contents

CHAPTER 1: VISION

The bomb wasn't a big one. It was only about a pound of C4 plastic explosive. It waited in the base of a concrete lamp-post on the outskirts of Belfast. One drizzly night a patrol of the Royal Marines wound it's way along the street. The IRA man was watching with binoculars, the radio detonator by his side. He waited till half the patrol had passed the bomb; he wanted to kill as many as possible. The man beside the blast had both legs torn off at the knee. His mates tried to tourniquet the ragged stumps but he died within five minutes in a pool of blood. The corpse twitched even after it was dead.

Captain Rod Jackson was blown several yards into a ragged, twisted heap. He convulsed as blood poured out of his mouth. He had over thirty fragments of steel and concrete in him. The surgeons saved him after three operations, but some small pieces remained inside him. The doctors thought that was OK, and if the fragments gave any trouble he could come back for further work.

Rod recovered and felt fully fit, but the Medical Board wrote 'Administrative Duties' on his file. He knew that was the end of a successful career in the Royal Marines. It would be a life of paper-pushing and making Major on time. It was the Corps' polite way of saying 'Quit while you're still young enough to do something else.' Rod took the hint and resigned his Commission. The day he left, he and a friend got drunk and swam the River Thames in full clothing. The River Police got them with a patrol boat and they were cautioned.

Several years later Rod was in London to attend a reunion lunch near the Tower of London. He had never intended to visit the Crown Jewels. He'd always thought the idea a rather touristy thing to do. But he had some time to kill so he wandered in to have a look. Besides, his family name gave him a kind of mild curiosity about the idea. He was Captain Roderick Blood Jackson, Royal Marines, Retired, distantly related to the famous Colonel Blood who in 1671 had so nearly made a successful attempt on the Crown Jewels. It was the custom in Rod's family to give all the sons the middle name of Blood to maintain the connection.

With the other tourists he rode slowly along the moving walkway which carried people past the jewel cases to stop them dawdling there. The egg-sized diamonds, almost too big to be true, slid slowly by. He stepped off at the end and moved to the raised viewing platform. He gazed round the room at the security cameras and thick steel doors.

Then the hairs on the back of his neck came up, and an electric thrill ran through his body. He tried to suppress the smile spreading over his face. He'd seen how to do it! It was so simple! There was a way.

He composed his features, feeling self-conscious standing there grinning. He hoped no one had noticed. The four biggest diamonds in the world were only a few feet away behind some glass, and he knew he could take them.

It was the tourists who had made this possible. The Crown Jewels used to be kept in an underground vault, but 15,000 people a day were trying to see them and this caused queues an hour long. So in 1994 the Queen opened a new Jewel House on the ground floor of the Waterloo Barracks.

It was the jewels now being at ground floor level which gave Rod the idea of how to take them. It was known that if an attack was made on the Jewel House the display cases containing the main pieces would lower automatically into the vaults below. Rod could see a way to overcome this.

The sudden vision that he could steal the Crown Jewels wasn't just a greed thing with Rod. His reasons were more complex than that. Sure, he could enjoy the wealth that would come from the jewels, but he wanted also to deal a blow to the monarchy which he had once served so loyally but had then thrown him on the scrap heap. To do this he needed the main regalia, the crowns and scepters, and above all the magnificent Stuart Sapphire. He'd been brought up as a Catholic but never taken it very seriously. Now approaching middle age some of the early teaching began to surface. The Germanic Windsor line of British royalty had crumbled to decadence in its standards, and almost unnoticed by himself, Rod had come round to a Jacobite point of view. If there was going to be a monarchy, then it ought to be the rightful one, the Stuarts. The line still existed in Europe with the strongest legal claim to the throne of Britain.

The Crown Jewels were a perfect challenge. Something exciting to do; a tricky operation to organize and pull off, yet feasible. It would be a blow, perhaps a death knell, to a crumbling and impostor royal house, and after a suitable cooling off period, the way to a fortune.

CHAPTER 2: PLANNING

Rod began to plan at once. Nothing was written down. No records were kept. It was all in his head. The first thing to do would be to put together a team, and keep it small. Rod lived in the county of Suffolk, about seventy five miles north east of London, near the North Sea coast. His home was in the village of Waldringfield, and he kept a boat there on the River Deben. He swam every day in the river or in the pool in the nearby town of Woodbridge. Swimming kept him fit and cleared his mind, and as he surged powerfully across the river to Stonner Island he was composing his ideal team for the attack on the Crown Jewels. Four in all would do it, and he would start with Mac.

Maclean was his surname, but he was always just Mac in the service. After a full tour in the Royal Marines he'd taken the Anchor pub at Felixstowe Ferry at the mouth of the River Deben. Mac was big, not above six foot, but broad and thick set. He'd grown a beard which gave him a fierce, scowling look. He wasn't cut out to run a pub. He'd made Sergeant in the Marines, and might have gone further, but he was given to brawling and insubordination. If Mac thought a plan was useless he said so. This didn't go down well with superiors, but Rod knew that if Mac backed an operation there was no one more loyal or determined to see it through.

Monday afternoon would be a good time to see Mac and take a walk on the beach. Rod knew that Mac was bored out of his skull with his present life. Being polite to customers he didn't like was a pain in the ass, and a real test of the little patience he had. Rod knew his plan would need careful selling. After a good lunch and some beer they took a walk along the beach.

Rod began with, "Mac, I've got a scheme worked out for a bit of action. There's a few risks involved, but no one should get hurt. What do you think?"

"You know me, boss, if it gets me out of this bloody routine I'm all for it. What's the job?"

Rod worked up to it slowly, "Well it would take you away from home for a bit. What would Molly think of that?"

"Bollocks to that, she's used to it. Anyway she's fed up with me griping about the pub and will be glad to see the back of me. We can easily get some help in."

"Well", said Rod, "The first bit's good. We're going through the Mediterranean and the Suez Canal to Bombay to collect some kit from there. How does that sound?"

Mac's face lit up, "Bloody magic! We had some good times in the Med, didn't we? Remember that Dutchman who broke a chair over your head in Malta? Bloody nearly killed you."

"Yeah, thanks Mac", said Rod ruefully as he rubbed the scar on his scalp, "He was aiming for you and I got in the way."

Mac laughed, "I had the bastard sorted but I had to carry you out and get you stitched up. You still owe me for a shirt, the blood never came out."

They crunched on through the shingle past the old Martello Towers from Napoleonic times as Rod detailed the whole plan.

Mac stopped, "You're bloody crazy boss, you know that, don't you? They'll never give up till they get you."

Now deadly cool, Rod replied, "Look, Mac, to get us they've got to find us, and you and I know enough about this game to get in, do the job, and get out again without leaving anything traceable. Think of it, a real challenge, loads of excitement, and all the money you can use for life. You can quit the pub and live in the sun anywhere you like. Molly would love that too."

They walked on in silence for a while, then Mac said, "Two conditions and I'm in. We don't kill anyone, and the others in the team have got to be ex-boots as well." Mac used the nick-name for Marines the world over, bootnecks or boots for short.

"Great, Mac, that's my feelings exactly. We might have to stun a few on the way in, but killing people isn't in the plan. And as for two more on the team, if they weren't boots I wouldn't take 'em on, you know that."

They stood and watched a car ferry pull out of Harwich harbor and head out across the North Sea to Holland.

Rod spoke quietly, "We trained all our lives for this, Mac. This is the big one. No one has all the skills like the S.B.S." Rod referred to the Special Boat Service to which they had both belonged. The equivalent of the Special Air Service in all respects, it was an ultra-tough elite from within the already elite Corps of Royal Marine Commandos.

A grin lit up Mac's features "You know, boss, you might just be bloody well right. It's the best thing I've heard in years. Count me in!"

"That's great, Mac. I know it's going to work OK. You know the form, we don't rush it, and we watch our security. Nothing written down and no phone calls. I'll come and see you when contact is needed, and if it's urgent you can come round to my place."

Mac nodded as Rod went on, "Can you be ready for the Bombay run in four weeks' time?"

"Sure, boss, I can be ready tomorrow if you want."

"OK, Mac, four weeks from today we'll set off from here, and I'll come and see you in three weeks' time for a briefing. And thanks, Mac, you won't be sorry. A year from now we'll be long gone into the sun."

They shook hands and Rod walked to his car. He liked four wheel drive for towing boats, and the Land Rover gripped well as he turned onto the winding road across the golf course towards Felixstowe

Over breakfast the next day Rod broke some news to his wife, Sue, "I'm going to grow a mustache, I need a change."

"Oh no, Rod, you'll look awful! Don't you remember how ghastly you looked when you grew a beard?"

"My mind's made up. I've got a new business scheme coming up and I need to look more mature."

Susan sighed, "Not another business scheme, Rod? Look how much we've wasted on your other projects."

"This time it's a loan, I promise you; an investment; you'll treble your money in a year."

She looked disbelieving, "That's what you always say, and they never work out. What's so good about this one?"

"Well it's a removals firm specializing in difficult cases. Me and some friends have found a niche in the market which no one else is doing, and we know it can work. Capital outlay isn't high either. It's something I can really throw myself into."

Susan remained skeptical as Rod added, "There is one thing though; I'll have to go abroad for a while to help set it up; shouldn't be too long."

"Oh darling, must you? I get so fed up on my own after a while."

Rod was soothing, "You've got your golf and your bridge, and you know me, I always come back, don't I?"

"Yes, I suppose so. Well if you think it will really work this time I won't stand in your way, but do be careful."

"Thanks, darling; it'll work out OK, you'll see."

Rod kissed her on the cheek and headed out for the car. Susan shook her head and sighed, but secretly felt relieved that Rod had at last found a scheme which seemed to fill him with enthusiasm. He had married well. She had an income from her family which kept them comfortably if not lavishly. It was the availability of this which had softened Rod's resolve in the various jobs he'd tried since leaving the Marines.

He drove to Birmingham, an easy 150 mile run along the A14 highway. In several shops he bought sunglasses of varying darkness and colors, and different styles of headgear, then added a selection of casual windcheater jackets. He paid cash for all the items and put them in a suitcase in the Land Rover. From newsagents he bought all the magazines relevant to the buying of second-hand yachts and boats.

Over the next few days at home he spent hours scanning advertisements and making phone calls. In the end he found what he wanted, a redundant fishing boat in good condition. There were plenty of these about. Commercial fishing was in a bad way as quotas were being cut back, and boats were being sold off at knock-down prices. Rod had always kept what he called his slush fund in banks in the Channel Islands, and had been feeding these with money steadily over the years. He transferred to a London bank more than enough for the first phase of his plan.

Thirty miles up the coast, Lowestoft harbor had that depressed, run-down look of so many declining fishing ports. Years ago it had been possible to cross the harbor there over the decks of the tied-up fishing boats. Now there were a few rusting trawlers, with morose crewmen sitting in harbor-side cafés remembering the good old days. Being on welfare didn't feed a family properly, and there was little other work in the town. Well, there was production-line work in the vegetable cannery, if you could call it work, but few fishermen could stand it for long.

Rod parked and walked into the old Eagle Café. He wore old, oil-stained jeans, a navy sweater out at the elbows, and an old yachting cap streaked with anti-fouling paint. The skipper of the motor fishing vessel, the Theseus, looked depressed. He was selling off his livelihood, and he knew that in middle age he would never go to sea again.

He and Rod walked along the quay to the boat and gave her a thorough inspection. She was only fifteen years old, sixty five feet long, and built in steel in the hopeful days when fishing quotas were good. She had the two things Rod was really looking for; heavy deck fittings in

9

tubular steel, and an eight cylinder Gardner 8LX diesel engine, the best of them all.

They talked prices and Rod beat him down with a cash offer well below the boat's real value. The ship's papers were in order, and Rod walked with the skipper over to the shipping office to get the sale formalized. Subject to final survey, the boat was his.

Johnson's, a local boatyard, was glad of the survey work; they were close to going out of business. Rod booked the boat to be hauled out, anti-fouled and painted with gray topsides. Her fishing license number was to be painted out but her name left on. The engine and winches were to be serviced, navigation and safety gear checked, and fuel tanks filled. Rod ordered several 50 gallon oil drums for the fish hold, and a hand pump and hose for transferring fuel from them to the boat's main tanks. Rod paid cash in advance, and got an assurance the boat would be ready in three weeks' time.

On the appointed day Rod collected Mac in a rental car and they made their way up the A12 highway to Lowestoft. The Theseus was ready and looked trim. The yard had done it's work well. Using the car they provisioned the boat from local stores for it's long return voyage. It was a cool, clear Spring day when they cast off and headed out into the North Sea, turning the boat south along the coast towards Dover and the English Channel.

CHAPTER 3: BOMBAY RAID

The sea trip out to Bombay went well. Rod and Mac soon got into a comfortable routine. The boat had radar, satellite positioning and an autopilot so navigation wasn't a problem. In the busy Dover Straits between England and France they were both on watch, but mostly they did the 'four on, four off' watch system which had worked for so long in the Navy. They soon settled into the sleep pattern this dictated. The Bay of Biscay was a bit lumpy but not too turbulent, and they plugged on at a steady nine knots to Gibraltar.

They refueled in Gib, and took a run ashore for a bath and a good meal in a hotel. Giving Malta a miss, Cyprus was the next port of call. They refueled in Larnaka, and headed for the Suez Canal. Both had been through before while serving on an aircraft carrier en route to the Far East. It needed both of them on watch to avoid the busy commercial traffic in the narrow channels. It was fascinating to see how even at low speeds the propellers of the larger ships churned sand off the bottom as they went along.

Nearing Bombay the talk focused more intently on the purpose of the trip. The key to stealing the Crown Jewels lay in two places in the world, Peru and India. Both nations had bought redundant large British warships and put them into service. The key was heavy naval shells. Both nations had retired their vessels now, but the guns and ammunition were stored ashore. The shells had a long storage life if kept in the right conditions. There was no way they could be bought openly. They would have to be stolen and smuggled back to Britain. India was an easier option for this than Peru. It was as simple as that.

Rounding Malabar Point and crossing Back Bay, the Theseus turned towards the port of Bombay. The port heaved with every kind of vessel in seeming disarray. Following radio directions from the Harbormaster, the Theseus tied up alongside a dock in the inner basin designated for visiting smaller craft.

Rod knew the form; leaving the boat unattended would be an open invitation to dockside thieves. He walked along the quay till he saw what he wanted. In a group of men chatting by some bales was a stocky little figure in faded khaki shorts and tunic. Hanging at his belt was the worn hilt and scabbard of the long Nepalese kukri knife.

Going up to the group Rod spoke politely but firmly to the small man, "You are a Gurkha?"

Rod pronounced it 'Goorkha' in the proper way. His English voice and tone of command had an instant effect.

The Gurkha sprang to attention and saluted "Sir!"

Rod did not offer to shake hands; he knew that was frowned on. He said, "I'm looking for a guard for my boat. Can you do this?"

"Yessir."

"Right, follow me", and the Gurkha fell into step beside and slightly behind Rod as they went back to the boat.

Rod got the details of the Gurkha's service in the British Army and inquired after his family in Nepal. His name was Khumde Duglha, and he was unmarried. He sent money back to his parents when he could earn enough.

Rod showed him over the crew's quarters in the bows. Handing Khumde a five pound note, Rod told him he would be night guard on the boat, and had one hour to return with his own choice of day guard. Khumde grinned broadly, saluted smartly and ran off down the dock. He was back within ten minutes followed by an even smaller but younger man also dressed in faded khaki.

"My worthless cousin, Sir, Chulhe Duglha. He is a good Gurkha also." Chulhe grinned two rows of perfect teeth and saluted smartly.

Rod addressed them both with military directness "Right, you cook your own food, and make sure there's always one on guard on the boat."

Both Gurkhas saluted smartly and walked forward chatting busily.

Mac had been watching all this from the wheelhouse. As Rod joined him Mac said, "Good move, boss, those little buggers will cut the balls off anyone who tries to get aboard."

Mac wiped his sweating hands on a piece of cotton waste and grinned at Rod, "I need a run ashore and a good screw; I'm starting to fancy you."

"Yeah, good thinking, Mac, I could do with one as well, but none of your back street stuff, we don't want to get a dose. We'll check into a hotel for the night and get some high-class skirt. We look a couple of scruffs, we'd better get cleaned up."

Half an hour later in clean slacks and shirts, and carrying an overnight bag, they left the boat.

Rod gave instructions, "Khumde, we'll be ashore for the night. No one is to come aboard. OK?"

"Yessir, the boat will be fine." He snapped to attention and saluted, then stood at ease in the proper military manner facing the dock.

Rod and Mac walked off the quay, hailed a cab and went to the nearest bank. There Rod bought rupees in quantity, then told the cab driver to take them to the best barber shop in town. Rod tipped the driver well and told him to come back in half an hour. The driver grinned, nodded his head sideways in the odd Indian manner, and drove away. Rod had let his beard grow on the voyage out, and they both looked like what they were, a couple of sun-tanned European mariners. The beard shaved off, they luxuriated in the shampoos and haircuts. The barbers took infinite care in the expectation of good tips, and were not disappointed.

Much refreshed, Rod and Mac boarded the waiting cab, and Rod said cheerily to the driver, "Take us to your favorite café and join us for a drink."

"Ah, thank you, Sir, I know a very good place."

The old Morris Oxford, a 1950's British design still made in India, rattled off through a maze of side streets. The café was small but clean, and had no other Europeans in it. Over cold bottled beer Rod found the driver was called Sanjiv and the café was run by his relatives.

Smiling pleasantly, Rod said, "Sanjiv, we're looking for a couple of good clean girls for the night, and a hotel which won't mind that. Can you help us?" Rod pushed a five pound note across the table as he spoke.

Sanjiv grinned, "Oh yes, I know some very good girls, very clean, very pretty; and the hotel you want is the Durbar, many Europeans, very discreet."

"Good. Fix up a time and place for us to meet the girls." Rod released the five pound note and Sanjiv palmed it expertly into a shirt pocket.

Rod then took out a ten pound note, put it on the table, and with a half smile devoid of humor said, "Sanjiv, my friend and I need some work doing in Bombay, a small removals job you understand. We need some men to do this for us, say half a dozen. It's a night job, not risky, and very well paid. So we need to meet someone who can organize this for us. We're not looking for a Mr. Big in Bombay, more like a Mr. Fix-it, someone with good contacts and connections. Can you help us there?"

Sanjiv eyed the ten pound note and licked his lips, "If it is drugs, Sir, I cannot do it, the penalty here is too high; I have a wife and children."

"No, don't worry, Sanjiv, it's just some equipment we need from a boatyard and the owners won't sell to us. It's a straight in and out job, no problems."

Sanjiv still looked nervous, "OK, Sir, I can find the person you want, but I cannot see him till later tonight."

"That's fine, Sanjiv", said Rod reassuringly, "Find out when and where we can meet him tomorrow, and leave a note at the hotel for us."

Rod pushed the ten pound note across to Sanjiv who palmed it smoothly into the same shirt pocket as he said, "Thank you, Sir, what names shall I put on the note?"

"Mr. Mare", Rod pronounced it 'Mar-Ray', "And Mr. Terram." He printed the names on a scrap of paper and handed it across. Mac grinned broadly on hearing the names. The Royal Marine motto was Per Mare Per Terram, By Sea And By Land.

Sanjiv knew the names were false but knew better than to push it "These are English names I have not heard before."

Rod smiled, "Yes, they're unusual, aren't they? But then our families were originally Italian you see. Come on, Sanjiv, let's get to those girls and the hotel."

They drained their glasses. Rod paid and tipped well, and they rattled off again in the taxi.

The next morning over breakfast in the hotel, Mac grinned, "Bloody 'ell, boss, that bird knew more ways of screwing than I do, and that's saying something! What a night, I'm knackered!"

"Yeah, bloody marvelous", agreed Rod, "But I'm not as fit as I was, I was only getting steam after a while!"

They tucked into a solid breakfast as Rod reflected that after a brief bout of torrid love-making he'd fallen into an exhausted sleep.

A poorly written note awaited them at the reception desk, 'Mr. Kapoor, 6pm, I will come to boat for you. Sanjiv.'

Rod paid the bills and left a good tip. The desk clerk with the greased down hair smiled knowingly, "Thank you, Sirs, do come again."

They took a taxi back to the Theseus, and walking up to her could see no guard. Mac muttered, "The little bastards!"

But just then a grinning face appeared round the wheelhouse, "Good morning, Sir!", said Chulhe as he snapped to attention and saluted.

"Thank you, carry on", replied Rod with a wave, and little Chulhe continued to pace importantly round the deck.

Rod and Mac changed into their sea clothes of jeans and denim shirts, and walked to the nearest dockside café, a seedy place with few Europeans, and seamen from half the countries in the world. Rod bought tea and they talked to the owner about competent boatyards round the docks.

Rod said, "I want someone who can do good welding work on tubular steel."

"Ah, you want the Bhatinder brothers, they're the best at welding steel on these docks. They're up at the far end near Ferry Wharf." He pointed up the dockside.

Rod and Mac walked along the docks, parallel to the P. D'Mello Road, till the bright splash of welding marked the small yard run by the Bhatinders. The two brothers looked like they were both made of rust. Their overalls and skin and hair were so full of red dust they had a sort of metallic patina. One kept on welding while the other walked across to speak to Rod. Middle aged and wiry, he looked like a shrewd man.

He began with, "What can I do for you?" There was no 'Sir', this was between equals.

Rod said, "I need some heavy steel tubes making up and installing on my boat, the Theseus, she's further down the dock."

"I can do that, but we're busy on a job as you can see. When do you want this doing?"

Rod frowned, "We need to move in two or three days' time. I can pay cash in pounds or dollars if you like."

Bhatinder was no friend of the English, and he could sense the urgency and the profit in it, "Dollars would be much better, but my client won't like me leaving this job, and he's a regular customer."

Rod could see this coming but he needed the work done, "OK I'll pay what you need to get the job done quickly."

Bhatinder nodded, "If you can bring your boat up here we'll start straight away."

Rod and Mac were sweating heavily by the time they got back to the boat, cast off, and moved her up to the Bhatinders' yard. Rod had made some drawings, and he explained in detail what he wanted as they walked round the boat.

All the tubular steel on deck was to be cut away and replaced by bigger diameter tubing. It had to be exactly seven inches in internal diameter, and entirely smooth inside with no welds or protrusions. The tubes were to be left open-ended but with end caps provided to be fitted later. Everything had to look old and original, not newly added.

Bhatinder listened intently, nodding from time to time, "The work is not difficult. Two men for two days can do this."

They agreed a price and Rod gave Bhatinder two hundred dollars as a first payment. "One more thing. I want you to cut six of these oil drums in half and weld a wide steel tube inside running from the filler cap to the bottom, then re-weld the drums very carefully so the joins can't be seen. And leave in the hold a complete welding set with full cylinders, rods and a face mask, OK?"

"All this I can do, and I know not to ask why you need steel tubes inside oil drums."

Taking the drawings, Bhatinder walked into his small office calling his brother after him. Two minutes later they reappeared, came on board and began to talk animatedly whilst pointing at all the tubular deck fittings. Then work started. A derrick on the dock swung across and chains were put round the stern gantry. Acetylene torches flashed as the steel was cut through. Rod and Mac could see the work was in good hands and needn't be watched constantly.

Rod called out, "Chulhe!", and the little Gurkha appeared from nowhere, "Sir!"

Rod said, "What would fifty good empty sacks cost?"

Chulhe hesitated, "I am not sure, Sir, I have never bought any, but I can find out."

"Here's fifty rupees to start with", said Rod, "Go and buy fifty good sacks and get them back here. Hire a hand cart if you have to."

Chulhe grinned and nodded at the same time, jumped ashore and ran off down the quay. Ten minutes later he was back, walking beside a hand cart pushed by a dockside laborer. The sacks were stowed away and the laborer was paid the balance of the money.

Rod and Mac prepared for their evening meeting with Mr. Kapoor. Each strapped a Fairbairn fighting knife in it's sheath to the inside of the left calf. Nothing showed outside the loose-cut slacks. Inside the waistband of the trousers, in a sheath centrally at the back, each stowed their own personal combat knife, the hilt above belt level and easily reached by either hand. The shirts, worn loosely outside the slacks, hung down over the hilts, concealing them completely.

Both knew exactly how to use knives to maximum effect. None of that film nonsense about knives in the back or stomach; that was all too slow, noisy and messy. A hand over the mouth from behind and a sharp backward pull as the blade was thrust upwards into the base of the skull and you were holding a rag doll.

Rod called Khumde on deck and gave him a five pound note as their second day's wages, then briefed him about their visit to Kapoor, "If we're not back by 0900 tomorrow, take Chulhe with you, find Mr. Kapoor and persuade him to tell you where we are. OK?"

Khumde's hand went down to the hilt of his kukri, "Oh yes, Sir, he will tell us."

Just then the taxi arrived with Sanjiv looking worried at having found the boat had moved. He thought his new-found benefactors might have gone. They boarded the taxi and left.

They had expected the meeting with Kapoor to be in some seedy part of the city, but were surprised to arrive in one of the better parts. Bhulabhai Desai Road was lined by well kept villas and apartment blocks, and it was at one of these that they stopped. Telling Sanjiv to wait, they went in the front lobby to find a small brass plate identifying Kapoor as being on the top floor. They took the elevator up, crossed to the door and rang the bell. A servant opened the door to admit them into a hall, then brushed past them to open a door to a spacious sitting room. French windows looked over a balcony and a stunning view to the island of Haji Ali's Tomb and the Arabian Sea beyond. A glorious sunset flooded the room with a pink glow. It was deliciously cool from the air-conditioning.

Kapoor came to meet them and motioned them to chairs. He wore a pale linen suit, and looked about thirty. He was of medium height and slim build, with intelligent, piercing eyes.

"Gentlemen, what can I offer you to drink? Whisky?"

They nodded assent and the servant placed a silver tray beside each of them. On these were crystal tumblers, ice cubes, soda siphons and unopened bottles of good whisky. Rod knew what whisky cost in India. This was no small-time crook they were dealing with.

"Well", said Kapoor, "You keep the Theseus well guarded, my boys are quite disappointed."

"You are well informed, Mr. Kapoor."

"Yes, I can usually have someone on board any boat in Bombay within a few hours of it docking. Sometimes there are good pickings to be had. People are so careless with their money and valuables."

Then, the pleasantries over, "Now, gentlemen, what can I do for you?"

Rod set out their exact needs, "We need a commodity which is not available on the open market. It has to be,

19

shall we say, liberated from it's owners. The commodity in question is six inch naval ammunition, specifically six inch caliber heavy armor-piercing ammunition; the semi-armor piercing won't do. You will know that the Indian naval warship the Mysore was de-commissioned some time ago, but her guns and ammunition are stored ashore at the Naval Depot up the coast towards Surat."

Kapoor's eyes had widened marginally, and he leaned forward slightly as Rod continued, "We need two things from you; a small team of men to carry out a break-in at the Naval Depot to remove at least twenty of these shells, and a special kind of person. We need a retired ex-Navy Chief Petty Officer Gunner who knows the layout of the depot, and who can identify there without fail what we're looking for."

There was a silence as Kapoor pondered his reply, "How interesting. A fascinating project. So different from the usual run of business one meets in Bombay. Mmm, yes, I think it can be done. I happen to know security is poor at the Naval Depot. The patrols carry .303 rifles and bayonets but are not trusted with ammunition. And I am not keen on shooting; the police become too interested."

He paused briefly, "It seems to me we need six men, a good truck, and your ex-Navy gunner. I take it you will not be part of this little venture?"

"No, we'll take the Theseus up the coast till we're just south of the Depot. We draw seven feet so we can't get too close inshore. You'll need a beach boat to ferry the load to us."

"Yes, that can be done. It will take me at least twenty four hours to make all the arrangements. When do you have in mind for this enterprise of yours?"

"The moon's low two nights from now, let's set it for then. But I must brief the naval gunner myself; he must know exactly what we need."

Kapoor was reassuring, "I am sure I can find such a man for you; there are many ex-Navy men looking for work. Their pensions are poor. Shall we say six tomorrow evening? But not here; too many people watch this place. I will send him by car to your boat."

"That's fine", said Rod. He poured himself another good whisky. Mac had already downed about a third of his bottle.

With a steely edge to his voice Kapoor said, "Now, about costs. I ask one thousand pounds for myself, two hundred per man involved, three hundred for the Navy man, and you supply the truck."

A tiny pause, then, "Payable in cash, in advance."

Rod knew of no other way; he looked across at Mac who gave a slight nod. Rod said, "Agreed, but on one condition. Your money in full now, but for the men, half now and half on delivery of the goods." He smiled, "All men need some incentive."

Kapoor understood entirely, "That is satisfactory. Deliver the truck tomorrow, not here but to this warehouse."

He scribbled a note on a small pad taken from an inside pocket and handed over the paper. Rod pulled a notecase from inside his waistband and attached to it by a chain, and counted out the money in new, high value notes. He handed the money to Kapoor who put it on the table without counting it.

He rose and said, "Thank you, gentlemen, that concludes our business. We will not meet again, and we have never met, have we? I trust your eventual use of the goods will bring you much profit. I shall not ask what it is, but I think I will watch the newspapers in the next few months."

Kapoor went towards the door which was opened from the outside by the servant without bidding. As Rod and Mac crossed the hall to the front door, Kapoor spoke with mildly reproachful humor, "By the way, gentlemen, there was really no need for the knives."

Mac scowled but Rod began to chuckle. Kapoor added, "He's good, isn't he?", inclining his head towards the servant, "He was the best pick-pocket in Bombay." Then the eyes went hard, "Besides, he carries a gun."

In the elevator Mac growled, "Sly bastard!"

"Shrewd though", said Rod, "He's young to be heading his own organization in a place like Bombay. He'll be Mr. Big round here one day."

"Yeah, if he bloody lives!", grumbled Mac.

In the taxi Rod said, "Sanjiv, join us for a meal at the best curry house you know, OK?"

They ate splendidly and drank well. Back at the dock Rod paid Sanjiv in rupees for the car's hire, then handed him a ten pound note, "You did well, Sanjiv, your introduction to Mr. Kapoor was most useful. At nine tomorrow, OK?"

Sanjiv grinned and nodded, "OK, Sir, nine o'clock."

He drove off happy. He was making more money per day than he sometimes made in a week.

Back on board Rod and Mac had a final Scotch apiece as they talked over the plan. Mac said, "Shouldn't be any problems, boss, except getting the stuff on board will be a bit of a bastard if there's a big swell running."

Rod replied, "We'll use a net hoist over the side with a tarpaulin in it, that should do the trick."

Mac nodded and they fell into their bunks. Sleep wasn't easy. The Theseus had been designed to keep her crew warm in cold north European waters. There were few vents in the steel hull and no fans. It was 90F during the day, and didn't fall below 80F at night. They lay in their own sweat and envied Kapoor his coolness.

What seemed like minutes later a huge crash of steel on steel woke them with a start. It was barely light and the Bhatinders were dropping heavy steel tubes on the deck.

Mac moaned, "Bloody hell! I need some sleep!"

Rod brewed coffee, knowing there was going to be no more sleep that day. The deck work was going well. The new, bigger tubing was being fixed in place. As specified, the steel was not shining new, but rust-pocked and faded with the patina of lying a long time in salt air. At nine Sanjiv arrived and Rod boarded the taxi alone.

"Today, Sanjiv my friend, you are going to buy a truck."

"Thank you, Sir, but I am a poor taxi driver and I cannot afford a truck."

"No, you idiot, for me! I need an ex-Army or ex-Navy truck, something like a Bedford 3-tonner or 4-tonner. Take me to where they are sold."

"OK, Sir, but the place is outside Bombay, on the road to Nasik, it will take an hour to get there."

"That's alright, let's go."

Rod watched fascinated as the cab climbed slowly away through Bombay's outskirts and into the foothills towards Nasik. Thirty miles out a big ramshackle dump of every kind of vehicle came into view. It was unfenced but had a sort of main gate with a hut marked Office just inside it.

"Go in the office, Sanjiv, and tell them you want to buy an ex-Army truck in good working order."

Sanjiv did this and reappeared with some keys, "They are down this way, Sir", he said, pointing.

The trucks were the worst Rod had ever seen. None would pass any sort of roadworthiness test in the western world. The least awful still had a good tarpaulin over the truck body, and the khaki paintwork was recognizable as ex-military. The engine fired after several attempts, but sounded rough. Blue smoke from the exhaust showed the piston rings were shot.

"OK, Sanjiv, they're all bloody awful, but at least this one is a runner. Go and buy it for the best price you can. Put it in your name."

Rod gave Sanjiv a bundle of rupees and waited till he came back with a receipt. The truck had cost a fraction of what Rod might have paid.

"Right, Sanjiv, we need a garage in Bombay which can work on this truck today. It has to be delivered by six o'clock tonight. Don't go more than thirty or I won't be able to keep up."

Like many service personnel, Rod had taken a truck driving course in the Marines, and the Bedford 3-tonner was familiar. But this one was virtually brakeless, and the gearbox was a nightmare. Sweat poured off him on the drive back, and threading through the back streets behind the taxi had Rod grinding the gears time and again as the lazy clutch failed to work properly. At last they swung into a small yard full of dead trucks and abandoned bus bodies. Sanjiv led Rod across to a tin shed from which came loud hammering sounds. An oil-stained old man and two youths in overalls were working on a chassis up on trestles.

Sanjiv said, "This is Mr. Guntakal. He is very good with all trucks."

Rod was in no mood for niceties, "I must have this truck roadworthy by five o'clock today. Bleed the brakelines and re-line the brakes if necessary. Put the clutch in working order, make sure the lights work, check the tire pressures and fill the fuel tank. If you can do this I will pay you well. If not, I will go elsewhere."

Mr. Guntakal walked slowly round the truck, eyeing it thoroughly, "If you drove it here, it is not so bad. Yes, I can do this. It will be ready by five."

Rod cheered up, "Thank you, Mr. Guntakal, I will see you at five."

Rod told Sanjiv to drive to the Naval Depot near Surat. It had a wire mesh fence surrounding it topped by three strands of barbed wire. There were floodlights at sparse intervals. A road with railway lines set in the tarmac led in through the main gate past a small guardroom where two sentries stood outside. Doubtless more were inside. The whole place did not look a great challenge. The problem would be locating where the key items were stored. Much would depend on the skill and knowledge of the ex-Navy man they hired.

Using Sanjiv's road map they explored the choice of routes towards the coast. They needed a road or track which reached the beach or nearly so, and which was little observed. None were ideal, but they found one eventually which would do the job. Several fishermen's huts were too close for comfort. Rod marked carefully on the map the chosen route. They retraced their way back to the Theseus.

The Bhatinders had made remarkable progress. The new tubular deck fittings were in place and being finished off by the brothers and two helpers. Chulhe watched impassively from the foredeck as Rod inspected the work. The new seven inch diameter tubing looked slightly out of scale with the rest of the boat, but it would pass scrutiny. Rod had briefed Mac to make sure he could use the welding gear OK, and he'd been practicing on the dockside. By four o'clock the work was done, and Rod and Mac satisfied themselves as to it's quality. Rod paid off the Bhatinders handsomely. He didn't want any loose tongues about which Europeans might have had such work done on their boat. Rod and Mac then moved the boat back to her berth in the dock.

Rod said, "Mac, here's a pile of rupees, go and buy a strong spring scale capable of weighing a full oil drum. I'm off for the truck."

With that Rod jumped into Sanjiv's cab and headed off down the dock. The truck was ready and Rod gave it a brief trial in the street outside the yard. It was transformed.

"Well done, Mr. Guntakal, she's fine; you've done a good job."

Rod paid him off and told Sanjiv to lead the way to the warehouse rendezvous. It was a dockside location up near the Jakaria Bunder Road, and several rough looking characters lounged about outside.

Rod took the keys out of the truck and looked round for an office. A small door opened in the larger warehouse door, and a tall, slim, rather purposeful looking Indian in brown overalls came towards Rod. He looked Rod up and down, and without speaking held out his hand for the truck keys. Rod handed them over and the Indian turned and walked back through the small door, motioning with his head for Rod to follow. They went up some stairs to an office. There Rod spread Sanjiv's map out on the table.

Rod said, "Low moon and high tide are just after midnight tomorrow. We will wait as close inshore as we dare at this point from midnight on." He pointed at the map, "This road and track get close to the beach. We will show a green light continuously towards the shore. We have no boat for moving the stuff from the beach to us. You will have to provide that."

The Indian nodded and walked out down the stairs and stood at the small door as Rod stepped through it and over to the waiting cab. The Indian hadn't spoken once.

Sanjiv said, "You are lucky, Sir, that is Jagdal, Mr. Kapoor's best man. He is called The Thinker. He does not make mistakes like others do."

"Doesn't talk a lot, does he?", said Rod.

Back at the boat it was nearing seven when a car pulled up and delivered a stocky, graying Indian. He seemed to have made an effort with his clothes, but one trouser knee was patched and the neck of his shirt was frayed.

Rod stood on deck and the Indian stiffened to attention as he said, "Permission to come on board, Sir?"

"Certainly, come aft", said Rod in a friendly way.

Sat in the cabin the Indian introduced himself as Chief Petty Officer Gunner Alwar.

"Hallo, Chief", said Rod warmly, shaking hands, "I'm the captain and this is my first officer."

Mac held out his hand, "Hi, Chief, nice to meet you."

CPO Alwar looked nervous, "I do not want to be here, Sir. I have never done anything like this before. But I am in much need of money. My wife is very sick, and I must support many in my family. That is why I do this."

Rod was sympathetic, "I understand, Chief, but don't worry, there's no risk involved. You'll be in and out very quickly."

"I hope so, Sir", said the Chief gloomily.

Rod gave instructions, "Now, Chief, I want you to write down exactly what we need, and stick to it without fail. Don't come away without the right stuff or the whole effort is pointless."

The Chief nodded, sensing the importance, and began to write on the pad provided.

Rod spelled it out carefully, "At least twenty rounds of six inch heavy armor piercing naval ammunition. It must be the base-fused heavy armor piercing stuff; the nose-fused semi-armor piercing won't do. Is that clear?"

The Chief nodded, "Yes, Sir, I understand."

Rod went on, "Fuses to go with the shells are vital as you know. The Type NH-70 if you can find them, if not, the NH-65."

The Chief wrote steadily as Rod added, "Also the propellant charges in their tubes with the igniters. Now, that's the core of the operation, if you can get more, that's a bonus. Also, as a decoy, try and take some smaller stuff, small arms ammo, anything you can find. The idea is to create the impression that the job was simply to remove some useful munitions. OK so far?"

"Yes, Sir, I have all that."

"Lastly, I want you to paint in white the words 'Free Kashmir' on at least two buildings inside the depot. I have the paint and brush for you here."

The Chief looked up as Rod said, "Right, Chief, read back what you've got."

He had it word perfect, "I know the depot well, Sir, it was my last posting before retirement three years ago. I was in charge of the ammunition storage, so unless they have moved the shells they should be where I last saw them. I hope so."

He still looked gloomy as Rod said, "You'll be fine, Chief, and don't forget, we're all depending on you. You have your money?"

"I have £150 and the same to come again I am told."

"That's right, and here's the paint and brush; don't forget to use it in the way we said."

Alwar took it and left in the waiting car. Mac muttered, "Gawd, he's a dismal piece of work! Do you think he's up to it, boss?"

"Yes, I think so. He's scared but he'll go through with it. Kapoor will see to that. At least the Chief is getting his money; I thought Kapoor would keep half of it."

That night Rod, Mac and Sanjiv had a final blow-out meal ashore at an excellent café Sanjiv knew. Rod paid him off well and thanked him for his help.

He was quite moved and made his own little speech, "It has been a good time for me, gentlemen. My son has made a little gift for you."

He took from a bag a tiny model boat carved in wood, a crude copy of the Theseus. It bore the name in scrawly writing 'Theseos'.

Up at six, Rod paid off the two Gurkhas. He wore his navy-blue peaked cap, and they paraded on deck with their few belongings. Coming to attention, Rod thanked them both, then gave each a ten pound note, "For your families", he said. "You have served me well. Dismiss!"

They saluted smartly and he returned the salute. They trooped off the boat and down the dockside at the rapid Gurkha light infantry pace, swinging their arms to shoulder level as they'd been taught. For a few moments they were proud soldiers again.

Rod and Mac re-provisioned the boat, paid their mooring fees, crossed to the fueling point and filled their tanks, then set out from the harbor. Heading first south, then round Malabar Point and north up the coast past Mahim Bay, they would be off the rendezvous just as it got dark. It was good to feel the sea breeze again after the stifling heat of the harbor.

Reading the depth sounder they crept in towards the shore. Rod called out, "OK, Mac, let go!", and in twenty

28

feet the boat swung at anchor in a light swell. They were less than a hundred yards offshore, and could clearly hear the waves breaking on the beach. They rigged a green light facing the shore and waited, There was nothing to do except wait and hope it all went well.

At 11 p.m. precisely four men cut their way through the boundary wire of the Naval Depot at the furthest point from the guardroom, and ran silently between the rows of darkened bunkers checking the numbers and symbols on the doors.

At 11.05 precisely a large fire blazed up on the far side of the Depot. Several guards ran shouting in that direction while others phoned for the fire trucks. In a time quick for India, two old fire engines, bells clanging, roared through the main gate already opened for them. The military truck close behind them had the word 'Fire' in large letters on both sides and long ladders on the roof, and was clearly part of the same convoy. The tall, uniformed driver swung it skillfully through the gates after the fire engines.

Massive bolt cutters made cheese out of the big padlocks on Bunker No. 32 and the steel doors creaked open. The Chief quickly checked by torchlight that the shells were correct and pointed to those needed. The men began to roll the heavy steel shapes along their wooden slats towards the door. The Chief and one other man ran to find the fuses and propellant charges in their respective bunkers. The truck had turned right when the fire engines turned left towards the fire, and guided by a torch signal, found Bunker 32. Two men began to load the shells into the back of the truck. The fire-raiser had run round the outside of the Depot to the break in the wire, then in and joined those at the truck.

Alwar reappeared, breathless, "We have found the charges and fuses, a hundred yards over there, Bunkers 42 and 60."

Jagdal ordered, "Stay here, Alwar. When we've finished loading, guide the truck for us."

There was a stifled cry of agony followed by muffled cursing. A dropped shell had crushed the bones of a man's foot like eggshells. He writhed on the ground clutching his useless foot, blood spurting through his fingers.

"Throw him in the back!", snapped Jagdal.

The Chief seemed rooted to the spot with fear. Jagdal cursed at him, "Get painting, you fool!"

The Chief ran to the truck's cab, pulled out the paint and brush, and began to scrawl 'Free Kashmir' on several bunker doors. He got almost more paint on himself. He threw down the paint and brush and climbed into the cab, shaking uncontrollably.

The tailboard banged shut and Jagdal jumped into the cab and started the engine, "Now guide us!" he hissed at Alwar.

Shouting, whistles, and the sound of running, booted feet got steadily closer as the long charge tubes were loaded. The boxed fuses were cradled carefully in sacking.

Jagdal gave the order, "Forget the other stuff! There's no more time! We must go now!"

He swung the truck back along their entry route and out past the startled guards at high speed.

On the boat Mac spoke quietly, "There's a boat coming down the coast towards us, sounds small."

In the binoculars they could make out an open launch. It came steadily nearer, then turned inshore and ran onto the beach. The only man on board cut the engine, jumped over the side and ran up the beach with a small anchor. He vanished quickly towards the fishermen's huts.

Truck lights swung into view towards the beach and went out. Reversing, the truck got to within a hundred feet of the water's edge before the wheels spun to a halt in the sand. The tailboard banged down and busy figures began to roll the heavy shells off the back. They hit the sand with a deep thud. The ladders off the roof, laid end to end, reached the water's edge. The shells were rolled along and heaved carefully into the launch. It's wooden bottom couldn't take all their weight in one go. It took three trips to complete the transfer to the Theseus.

Rod worked the hydraulic winch powered by the boat's main engine, and swung the netted rounds into the hold. Mac, sweating and cursing, rolled the heavy shells out of the tarpaulin and wedged them into place. On the third trip Jagdal came out with the last of the shells and tied up alongside briefly, rising and falling in the swell.

"Money", was the only word he said.

Rod went to the wheelhouse and returned with the wads of notes in rubber bands. He handed them down to Jagdal who pushed them into his shirt without counting them, and the small craft turned away.

An old Peugeot pick-up drove out of a thicket, the men scrambled on and it disappeared up the track. Seconds later a ball of fire lit it from behind as the truck exploded in flames.

Rod yelled, "Let's get out of here, Mac! Get the anchor up!"

The blaze from the burning truck lit them up perfectly. As the anchor cleared the water Rod gunned the big Gardner diesel and swung the boat out to sea. Ten knots was their best speed without melting the main bearings, but due west they would be fifty miles into the Arabian Sea by dawn.

At noon the next day they eased up and came back to half speed to steady the motion.

Rod said, "Let's check the load, Mac, and see what we've got. We've got a lot of work to do."

They aligned the boat nose-on to the swell to minimize rolling, and the autopilot held them steady on course. They counted twenty two of the heavy shells, twenty four propellant charges and igniters, and twenty four fuses in two boxes of twelve.

Rod was pleased, "Bloody good; that Jagdal pulled it off."

Mac grumbled, "Yeah, but they've been soaked in sea water and they're covered in sand."

Rod was businesslike, "OK, Mac, let's get to work, we'll clean them, grease 'em up, and get them in their tubes."

Each six inch shell was wrapped in sacking till it was an easy push fit inside the seven inch steel tubes on deck.. Flexible jointed rods were used to push the shells into place. The big shells went into the deck tubes, and the lighter propellant charges went into the transom gantry and outriggers. The boxed fuses went into the cabin to await hiding later. It took till dark to get it all done, and they were both exhausted.

"Time for a couple of beers, Mac; we'll have to leave the welding till tomorrow; can't risk it in the dark."

Next day the welding was slow work. Rod played a hose on the steel tubes as Mac carefully welded the end caps into place. They daren't risk too much heat on the sensitive stores inside. At last it was done, and the welds red-leaded and painted to look the same as their host metal.

Talking over the raid in the cabin that evening, Mac reckoned it had been a success.

Rod was cautious, "Yes, on the surface it's OK, but I'm worried about one thing."

"What's that, boss?"

Rod spoke quietly, "Well, you see, Mac, this load is a bit of a giveaway. Anyone who steals this lot knows exactly what they're going to do with it. You can't free inland Kashmir with a load of heavy naval ammo."

In London, Superintendent John Cooper had just come to exactly the same conclusion.

He worked in F4 Division, Prevention of Terrorism, Metropolitan Police, Scotland Yard. Interpol reports of explosives thefts from all over the world routinely crossed his desk. Most of them involved Semtex from Libya, dynamite from quarries, and similar events. Northern

Ireland was always high in the Division's priorities. No one who had seen the file on the Bombay raid before him had commented in writing over some Indian extremists stealing the wrong stuff from an arsenal, when all around them was a pile of much more useful material. Typical bungling amateurs it was assumed.

But John Cooper was interested, because it was odd, and odd things stuck in his mind. It was too precise. The shells with the right fuses and the right propellant charges. But who the hell in the way of a terrorist group had the guns to fire them? No one fitted the bill. Oh well, it was probably some Middle Eastern oddballs anyway, and too far away to be a Divisional concern. He wrote 'File' on the docket and put the folder in his out tray. But he didn't forget it.

Odd fish, the Superintendent; not a street man, definitely a files man. He had served in the Royal Air Force as a weapons engineer, then gone to university to study modern history. Joining the police gave a good outlet for his powers of meticulous analysis and fastidious attention to detail. But he wasn't popular on the police force. He was on the team but not a real team player, and had made few friends. His record was good but he wasn't going any further.

In the Arabian Sea, Rod gave the island of Abd el-Kuri a wide berth. Owned by Yemen, pirates plied these waters. The two 12 gauge pump-action shotguns in the wheelhouse were loaded with buckshot, deadly for a short range fight. But if they got shot-up from a distance by .50 caliber or 20 mm cannon fire from a bigger vessel, they'd had it. Re-fueling at Aden gave no problems, and they pressed on up the Red Sea past the Dahlak Islands and headed for Port Sudan. It was there the danger lay because they had to buy more weapons.

Rod and Mac swam daily from the boat, pacing it at low speed till they'd had enough. One watched for sharks while the other swam. Gradually they got their service fitness back. Both were well tanned and felt good. They talked long about the plan for London and the taking of the Crown Jewels from the Tower, and refined it steadily. The first job back home would be to choose the other two to join the team. Rod and Mac had got the short-list down to four likely prospects.

They timed their arrival into Port Sudan for 8 a.m. The harbor was a shambles, and a small vessel flying a British flag was a rare sight. The Harbormaster's voice crackled abruptly over the radio, there was no greeting.

"British vessel, how long is your stay?"

"Estimated twenty four hours, thank you."

"Proceed to Pier 3 and await Customs inspection."

A Customs Officer with a holstered pistol, and four soldiers with Kalashnikov AK47's boarded the boat.

"Where you from?", demanded the Officer.

"From Aden", replied Rod calmly.

"And before that?"

"Bahrain; we're divers working for BP in the Gulf."

The soldiers opened the hatch over the fish hold,

"What is in the drums?", demanded the official.

"Diesel; we can't get home without the extra range."

The officer seemed dissatisfied that he hadn't found any reason for a fine or impounding the boat, and waved his men ashore.

"Cheerful lot, aren't they?", said Rod.

"Assholes!", replied Mac and spat over the side.

"Mac, it's too risky for us to move in the town alone at night. I'll trade by day, with you on guard here, and we'll both stay on board overnight."

Rod went below for currencies, reappeared with a small satchel, and climbed the ladder up the pier wall.

He turned, "If I'm not back by dark, bugger off on your own, Mac."

"Piss off!", said Mac with cheerful emphasis.

Rod grinned and hoisted himself onto the dock. It was already too hot.

He hailed the first taxi he found and told the driver to take him to the Soukh. The evil-looking greasy-haired driver feigned ignorance, "I do not understand, Sir."

"You know, where the action is."

"Ah, yes", smiled the driver.

They headed off down a succession of ever narrower side streets.

The driver muttered something incomprehensible into his radio, and two minutes later the taxi swung into a small square. The car seemed to be driving straight at a garage door. It flew open and the car was in, stopped, and the door shut in seconds.

Inside the small satchel Rod's hand let go of the firing lever on the smoke grenade as he kicked open the door on his side smashing it into the face of the man bending towards it. Rod was out as he threw down the grenade and drew his knife with his right hand. Behind him a man came round the car with a short iron bar. Rod kicked him in the balls and he fell screaming. Choking orange smoke rapidly filled the small garage as a third man lurched towards Rod with a long curved knife held point down. Rod kicked up against the arm smacking it into the side of the car as he swiped his own blade down across the inside of the man's elbow opening it to the bone. He reeled back cursing and gouting blood.

Killing these amateurs would be easy, but dead locals could cause police trouble, so choking on the bitter smoke, Rod kicked open the garage door, stumbled into the square and broke into a run.

Two streets later he walked calmly into a wider avenue with shops on both sides. Open-fronted cafés had people drinking coffee and their morning bracers over the newspapers. It was almost civilized. Rod sat at the smartest looking café and ordered coffee. He studied the occupants slowly, all men. After a few minutes one rather dapper, middle aged man folded his paper carefully, finished his coffee and rose to go. Rod followed him discreetly down the street and saw him enter a glass-fronted office. The sign said in French and English 'Dessie Tokar, Accounting Services'.

Inside, Rod found a fat girl sitting at a typewriter and filing her nails. It was not a busy office.

"Mr. Tokar, please", he said.

"Name, please?", she said with indifference.

"Mr. Bijoutier", said Rod with a smile. He couldn't resist giving the French for jeweler.

The girl opened a door marked Private and reappeared moments later, "Mr. Tokar will see you now, Sir."

The office looked dusty and unprosperous; a man who could do with some business.

Tokar rose, "Come in, Mr. Bijoutier; sit down please. An unusual French name for an Englishman."

"Channel Islands, Mr. Tokar; many of us from there have French sounding names."

Tokar knew enough about banking to know that the Channel Islands held much wealth. This Englishman might be a good prospect, "Ah, I see. How can I help you?"

"I'm starting a business here importing hydraulic machinery; my ship is in the harbor now; and I need someone who understands the trading patterns here to handle all my accounts." Rod thought 'ship' sounded better.

Tokar warmed visibly, "Certainly, Mr. Bijoutier, we are a long established and well respected firm. Also I know personally all the important officials from whom one must obtain the necessary licenses, you understand." Tokar thought the 'we' might disguise his one-man operation.

"That's fine, Mr. Tokar. I'd like to open an account with you; shall we say advance expenses?", and Rod spread £100 in new £10 notes on the desk and made sure Tokar saw the billfold containing many more. Tokar's eyes widened. No one paid in advance here. You were lucky to get paid at all, and then in worthless local currency. This Englishman was a gold mine.

"Certainly, thank you very much." Tokar slid the notes into his desk drawer and locked it. The girl had sticky fingers.

Rod said, "Good, let's make a start over early lunch then, Mr. Tokar. You will be my guest, I hope?"

"Certainly, Mr. Bijoutier, and thank you. May I suggest the Hotel Assab; their food is excellent." It was also a place he could never afford to frequent.

Rod replied, "I look forward to it. At twelve in the restaurant. Would you ask your staff to call a taxi for me please?" Rod thought 'staff' was a flattering way to refer to the slovenly girl.

Tokar snapped something at her and she crossed the street to a café where a local driver took his refreshment. A minute later the cab appeared.

Rod said, "By the way, Mr. Tokar, I need twenty five bags of dry, fine sand; oil spills in the engine room, you see. Where can I get these?"

Tokar contained his surprise, "Rhandaq the builder can do that for you, on the Atbara Road."

"Would you direct the driver for me please?" This Tokar did, and Rod ended with, "Until twelve then, thank you and goodbye."

Rhandaq knew already that all Westerners were crazy, but the British became top of his list. In a place where limitless sand could be had for free, this Englishman would pay hard currency for it. Rod was insistent that it be fine, dry and powdery, and demonstrated the point.

At the Hotel Assab well before twelve, Rod ordered bread and butter and milk. His stomach would be well lined before the alcoholic blitz about to hit it.

Tokar could not recall a better meal. The aperitifs, chilled wines and brandies glided down. He hardly realized that by 2 p.m. Rod had promises that Tokar would help him with certain 'trade contacts' that afternoon. By 4 p.m. Rod had paid cash in U.S. dollars, half down and half on delivery, for eight Russian-made RPG-7 rocket grenade launchers and twenty white phosphorus hand grenades, and was back at the boat, while a taxi returned the now sleeping Tokar to his office.

On seeing Rod on the quay, Mac called up, "Hey, boss, some friggin' rag-heads with a truck just dumped a load of sand in sacks up there, and kept jabbering and pointing down at the boat."

"That's OK, Mac, they're ours; let's get 'em loaded." He jumped down the ladder and they got the derrick working.

"And there's some other stuff coming too, Mac, RPG's and grenades. As soon as we've got them, let's push off. I had to drop some guys in a scrap this morning and their buddies will be looking to settle the score."

"OK, boss, suits me."

The RPG's and grenades arrived at dusk in an old van. Rod and Mac checked all the weapons carefully, the seals were in place and unbroken. The balance of the cash was paid, and the Theseus cast off. It was just dark as she slid away out of the harbor. The taxi containing four men, one with a bandaged arm, and all carrying Kalashnikov AK47's, arrived as they turned the point.

For the next two days towards Suez, Rod and Mac worked steadily on deck. A drum full of diesel was weighed carefully. They cut the tops off several oil drums just below the rim. Into these drums went the rocket grenade launchers, the phosphorus grenades, and the shell fuses, all carefully wrapped in plastic and tightly taped. The drums were re-filled with fine sand till their weight matched exactly those full of diesel fuel. The tops were re-welded on with great care, then the welds buffed smooth till invisible, and painted over. The tubes under the filler caps were filled with diesel. If the drums were dipped by Customs inspectors, they would show only oil right to the bottom. They ditched the welding equipment, spare sacks and sand over the side.

The return transit of the Suez Canal gave the temptation to visit the brothels of Suez or Port Said, or even a side trip to Cairo. But the Queen left for her summer holiday at Balmoral in Scotland by the end of July, and it was essential for her to be in London for the success of Rod's plan, so the Theseus plugged on at her best speed.

The Mediterranean was still fairly cool in early summer, but Rod and Mac kept up their daily swims, extending these gradually till they could do an hour hard without fatigue. Swimming was a key part of the plan, they weren't doing it for fun. They re-fueled at Larnaka, and again at Gibraltar. The Bay of Biscay played up with an early summer storm which cut their speed back for a while, but by the Pointe de St. Mathieu it had blown itself out.

It was part of their cover plan to collect some date-marked bills from France, so a night in a Cherbourg hotel was most welcome, and again at Boulogne and Calais. Crossing the Dover Straits into the Thames Estuary, they picked up a mooring at Queenborough on the west of Sheppey Island. They went ashore for a meal and a drink, and Rod phoned ahead to St. Katherine's Dock by Tower Bridge for a berth the next day. Yes, they had space, and high tide was about midday.

The trip up the river to the Thames Flood Barrier was uneventful, but from there on up, both scanned the banks carefully for places which were relatively quiet and not flanked by apartments or other housing. These quieter spots Rod marked carefully on a large scale map. He shaved, retaining a trim mustache, and he and Mac dressed in more colorful gear suited to the yachting fraternity.

Picking up one of the yellow buoys at the entrance to St. Katherine's Dock, they waited till the lock gate opened, then moved through with some other craft. Directed to a berth, Rod nudged the Theseus deftly into place, using the sideways push of the single screw to edge the stern against the pontoon.

Rod had seen the Customs man in his office eyeing them keenly as they came past, and expected a visit. Sure enough, some minutes later he arrived, civility itself. Travel-stained trawlers were not a common sight among the plush yachts and glitzy cruisers. Rod and Mac both felt a frisson of tension as the Customs Officer stepped up onto the Theseus from the pontoon. Benign and smiling, he was infinitely more dangerous than the crude, gun-swinging soldiers in Port Sudan.

"Good day to you, Sir. Where are you from?"

"From the Medway last night, and before that France", said Rod with the satisfied air of a sailor who has 'gone foreign'.

"Whereabouts in France?", asked the official pleasantly.

"Cherbourg, Boulogne and Calais", smiled Rod.

"And your home port, Sir?"

"Lowestoft."

"Would you mind opening the hold please?"

"No, certainly", and Mac obligingly opened the hatch. The cases of French wine and beer were evident but not too copious.

"What's in the drums, please?"

"Some are empty and some have diesel in. I'm not paying French prices, they have to pay tax on their marine diesel, you know." Rod feigned indignation at the prospect of having to do this.

"Just open two or three up for me will you? Those two and this one."

The official pointed at three widely spaced drums. He climbed down the ladder after Mac, who used a flat iron bar in the grooves of the filler caps to undo them. One was empty and the man shone a small torch into the opening. The other two contained weapons and sand, but oil showed up to the filler neck. Rod could feel the beads of sweat forming under his mustache. The Customs Officer kicked each drum in turn with a rubber-soled shoe and got the reassuring thud of a full drum. He bent down and wiped a finger across a small diesel spill.

"OK, that'll do. Thank you, and have a nice stay."

"Sure, we're going to hit the town tonight", said Rod rather too cheerily so it didn't ring quite true.

The Customs man walked off down the pontoon and Mac exhaled hard, "Phew! That bastard had me going!"

"Yeah, he suspects something, but he's thinking drugs, not what we've got."

They both went below for a stiff drink. Meanwhile in his office the Customs man filled in his Log: Theseus, Motor Fishing Vessel, ex Medway, Calais, Boulogne, Cherbourg. Home Port, Lowestoft. Under 'Comments' he wrote: 12 drums in hold, diesel. Very fine sand underfoot; been ashore?

He rubbed a finger and thumb together, and mused quietly, "That's really fine and powdery; I don't know any place in the UK that has sand as fine as that."

Mac spent the night on board while they talked over again their list of possible team members. They had a good meal ashore at one of the dockside restaurants, and Rod bought drinks for several other people there, establishing an amiable character for himself, and one not short of funds.

The next morning Mac set off for his pub in Suffolk, "It's been great, boss, just like old times. It'll be hard to settle down again."

Rod shook his hand, "Thanks, Mac, you know you're a key part of the team, don't you; it doesn't work without you. Here's a grand for your help." Rod gave Mac £1,000 in cash and he seemed almost reluctant to take it.

"Ta, boss, can't wait for the big one."

"I'll be in touch soon, Mac; keep fit, and don't let Molly see that!"

"Fat chance!", laughed Mac as he stepped down onto the pontoon, which sagged under his bulk, and walked away.

It was June 13th. For two more days and nights Rod continued gently and not ostentatiously to build up his image as a convivial and experienced sea-going yachtsman. He began to make friends among the like-minded people who lived long-term or permanently on their yachts in the basin, and there were quite a few of these. He asked some to drinks in the small cabin of the Theseus, and could always offer good malt whiskies, fine Armagnac and good cigars. In turn he began to be invited back onto other boats, some of which were spacious and luxurious in every detail.

In the next few weeks Rod took care to be on board two or three nights a week, and had established himself firmly as persona grata among the fraternity in the basin. He was seen as a sound man, not a bullshitter, and someone you could rely on. He was a Brit too, which was a relief when half the visitors came from God knows where, stayed ten minutes, and acted like they owned the place.

CHAPTER 4: PREPARATION

By phoning from home Rod found out the main State Events on the calendar that summer. There was the Trooping of the Color on the Queen's Official Birthday; a State Visit to Britain by the King and Queen of Thailand in return for one made to that country by Elizabeth II; and the last event was to be a State Visit to London by the President of Egypt. The dates set for this were Friday 25th July to Monday 28th July. Shortly afterwards the Queen would go to Balmoral in Scotland for several weeks.

Carefully Rod checked through the tide tables for London. Excellent! High tide occurred close to midnight on Saturday 26th July. That would be it then, attack time! Rod's pulse quickened and he smiled grimly.

There was much to do. He drove to see the four short-listed ex-Marines he and Mac had chosen. The problem of selection solved itself. The first one had damaged his back on a construction site and could barely move. The second one liked the sound of the action and the money, but hated Mac's guts.

"No, boss, not with that bastard Maclean. He got me busted from Corporal for being in a fight he started. Nah, if Mac's involved you can shove it."

But ex-Marine Mike Corder was on hard times, and went for the scheme right away. A tough little boxer, complete with broken nose, he worked as a trainer at a small gym at Catford in south London, and lived in two rooms above it. A brief outline of the essentials, the sight of £1,000 in cash, and the promise of at least a million in a year's time were more than enough. Rod liked the little Marine, and knew he could rely on him to be close-mouthed until contacted again.

Bill Harding took some persuading. He was doing alright. He'd become a salesman for a carpet company and was making quite good money. Rod's idea appealed though, and Rod knew if he was going to swing it, it would be the money angle which worked.

"What do you do with your money, Bill?"

"The wife spends most of it, doesn't she? Can't ever get enough; new fridge, new TV, new furniture, never friggin' ends!"

Rod said quietly, "Well, a million will give you both a plush villa in Spain, or where you like, and all the money you'll ever need. What are your chances of winning the lottery?"

"Sod all as far as I can see."

"Well, I can guarantee you a lottery win. Where the hell are you going to get an offer like that?"

"When you put it like that it makes sense. And anyway I'm getting fed up grafting for a living. I'm about ready for lying back on a beach." Bill paused, "And if it shuts the wife up, so much the better! OK, boss, count me in."

"That's great", said Rod warmly, and they shook hands.

Rod gave him a stern warning about security, not even a slight hint to his wife about their life getting much better before too long.

Pocketing the £1,000 in cash, Bill said with a big grin, "She'll see bugger all of this!"

The next day Rod paid cash for a second-hand typewriter in the town of Colchester, well away from his home. The typewriter was electric, the sort which still had keys to strike letters onto the paper. This machine had to do a better quality job than most ink-jet printers. Going on to the town of Maldon, he visited an ex-Marine friend who ran a small printing business.

"Morning, Tom", said Rod, "I need a little job doing. It's a joke some friends and me are pulling on a couple of snooty neighbors near us. We're going to send them some fake invites to a big garden party. It'll be a bloody good laugh when they turn up. Can you do a few sheets of this logo on your best paper?"

Rod handed over a sheet with the words Buckingham Palace typed in small capitals near the top.

Tom looked doubtful, "I don't want to get done for this."

"Relax, there's only two of them, and the sheets are quite untraceable. It needs to be in small capitals, embossed in maroon, and not on white paper, it's a sort of pale cream vellum."

"Yes, I know the stuff, but embossing is pricey for short runs; the cost is in the setting up; it gets cheaper the more you do."

"The cost doesn't matter, Tom; I'll give you cash and you needn't put it through your books, OK?"

"Well, I suppose so, but we're busy for the next week; it's not urgent, is it?"

"No, in a week's time is fine, and I'd like a few envelopes of the same stuff. Give me a call when they're ready and I'll come and get them."

A week later Rod typed two letters with great care, and wearing thin plastic gloves, he folded the letters neatly into their envelopes. These went into his briefcase. The typewriter he took outside and put on his drive. He drove over the typewriter several times, reversing to and fro till it was well crushed. The pieces went into a strong plastic bag. He drove the five miles to the Foxhall Road waste disposal site near Ipswich and threw the bag into the appropriate bin. The typewriter pieces would be in a crusher within days, compressed invisibly into a cube of other waste metal.

The Bedfordshire Firework Company was famous; they did all the big displays. Wearing pale blue rimless glasses, a baseball cap and a bright yellow windcheater jacket, Rod ordered an expensive array of fireworks for a big summer party he was giving at his country house. There were many tall trees so the fireworks had to be mainly aerial.

And there was going to be a noisy rock group so the fireworks had to be mainly loud bangs, the louder the better, the colored stars and festoons would be a bonus. The extra-loud mortars known as maroons which made a specially impressive boom were ordered in quantity. No, it was alright he assured them, there were no neighbors nearby to be disturbed. Rod paid cash, all in new notes from an impressive billfold, and yes, he would collect the fireworks in two weeks' time. Still chewing gum, he climbed back into the too obvious crimson Bentley Turbo convertible and drove away.

The return rail journey Rod made to Falmouth in distant Cornwall was an all day job. Mac, Bill and Mike had provided their own exact measurements, and with his own, Rod ordered from Cornish Diving Enterprises four hand-made wet suits. They were unusual in that they had to be matt black and not shiny. Gloves and hoods were included. Gear such as weight belts, swim fins and masks went in too. Having been paid cash the firm would be glad to mail the whole order to the accommodation address in London they were given. Nice guy, they thought; knows his stuff, but still diving with an eye patch might be a problem.

The breathing apparatus was harder. It had to be the closed circuit recirculating type which didn't leave a trail of bubbles. Again, an ex-Marine contact proved useful. The Submarine Museum in Gosport had on it's staff a retired Marine with whom Rod had served. Yes, the sets were still obtainable, though expensive. They were ordered infrequently by people who worked in aquaria where streams of bubbles disturbed shy breeds of fish, and by underwater wildlife photographers who needed close-ups of insects and pond life. Wilson Apparatus of Swindon made the equipment, and they were duly visited by Rod. Yes, they could do them from stock, and were pleased with such a good order. To be paid in cash was a bonus. They were put carefully in the back of the old Renault van with the Welsh license plates. Rod's heavy, horn-rimmed glasses, the pipe, and the hesitant, absent-minded manner had left a suitably academic impression.

The big-breasted sales girl in the yacht chandlers thought this man in the yachting cap, pale sunglasses and navy jacket was a mite stupid, and it showed in her voice, "Black rope? No, Sir, I haven't seen any of that. Our customers prefer the brighter colors, you see. They use different colors for each job on their yachts, red for one, green for another, and so on."

Rod examined all the ropes carefully. There was one of a suitable gauge and suppleness in dark navy blue.

"How much would you like, Sir?", she simpered.

"I'll take the whole roll", said Rod, paid cash and left.

Sales of ex-military equipment of any size, such as vehicles and boats, took place at Ruddington in Nottinghamshire, some 200 miles from Rod's home. Checking by phone, he noted the date he needed. Renting a suitable boat trailer, he drove up on the appropriate day. The dealers in surplus supplies bought in lots, and Rod knew he couldn't compete in that way. Asking around, he found the man the dealers had ringed between themselves to get the boats and engines, and told him what he wanted. This was a craft known as a rigid raider, a tough aluminum hulled open assault boat capable of carrying a squad of fully armed men and their equipment, plus two Evinrude 40 hp outboard motors in good condition to go with the boat. The offer of cash on the spot did the trick. Rod knew he'd paid over the odds, but he came away with his pick of the boats and motors.

On the drive back, the Land Rover developed a slow puncture in the right rear tire; there was a mess of metal scrap in the sale area and Rod had inevitably driven over some.

He cursed, "Sod it! And it would be raining!"

The wheel nuts were stiff and it took some time to change the wheel. In a foul mood he threw the flat tire in the back of the car and drove on. He made a long detour to drop off the outboards at an Evinrude dealer a hundred miles from home. The boat went into a hired farm shed in mid-Suffolk, later to be re-sprayed from it's khaki to a matt black inside and out.

Collection of other equipment went on steadily. None of it came to Rod's address; all was bought by cash. Body armor, smoke grenades, gas masks, the guns which fired the solid baton rounds used by riot squads, ex-service rucksacks, diving watches and wrist compasses, handcuffs, CO_2 extinguishers, crowbars; the list was long but eventually complete.

Rod took special care over a device he made in his garage. It was a dummy six inch shell, complete with propellant tube behind it. It was in wood, exactly to size, and hollow so it could be seen right through. Inside he fitted a hunting rifle telescopic sight, mounted right at the back. The sight had a long eye relief. When he put his eye behind the 'scope, the cross-hairs would show exactly where the gun barrel was aligned. He wrapped the dummy shell and stowed it carefully in a long piece of thick plastic tubing, taped over at both ends.

The equipment was ready. What was needed now was a decoy car. It had to be flashy, the flashier the better. He thought at first of a bright red Mercedes, but settled on a white BMW well past it's sell-by date. Parking round the corner from the little south London garage, Rod pulled on some oil-stained overalls, a greasy cap, and stuck a cigarette butt behind his ear. Strolling up to the garage owner, Rod enjoyed haggling with him.

Walking round the white BMW, Rod began with, "Look, mate, I don't mind if it ain't legal, I only want it for a week-end. All I need is a quick motor which won't blow up on me, know what I mean?"

Suitably hurt, the man countered with, "Ain't legal? Do me a favor! I don't touch bent motors. It's quick alright, been round the race tracks, that 'as."

"Yeah, ten friggin' years ago", scorned Rod. "Cash in hand then, what are we talking about? And it stays here till I need it in two weeks' time."

"It's on me books for a grand, but for cash now, seven 'undred and fifty."

"Seven hundred and it's a deal", said Rod.

"Done!", replied the dealer.

And Rod knew he had been. But he needed the flashy car. It was part of the plan. He counted out the cash in soiled used notes, and the man counted them again. Rod took the keys, saw the tank was filled, and arranged to collect the car on Saturday 26th July.

Taking the butt from behind his ear and lighting it, Rod said, "I'm looking for some likely lads to do a small driving job for me; nothing dodgy, it's a decoy run, the cops will be going the other way."

The garage man felt obliged, having just sold Rod a cut and shut car, "You want the Green Man pub in Commercial Way, down to Peckham. Go after nine and tell Mick behind the bar that Barry sent you."

"Ta, mate", said Rod, and slouched round the corner.

So it was that evening that Rod found four young men in the pub, and after suitable and careful inquiries, the purchase of copious drinks, and the production of cash, to do the driving job for him. Half the cash down, and half to be waiting at the other end. No, it wasn't drugs or guns, it was just a decoy run to throw the cops off another job. No, they hadn't got police records they said; well, nothing serious, just minor stuff. Rod gave them simple instructions and checked that they understood. The keys would be waiting with the car.

The next day Rod toured the south London areas of Rotherhithe and Deptford. The local health authority had kindly provided a list of the registered retirement homes. Yes, they were sure he'd find one which suited his dear old mother. Checking them all, he found what he wanted; one close to the River Thames, and on a street with double yellow lines setting out a strict no-parking zone. The lines were important.

A week from the deadline Rod called a meeting in London of the team. They had a good lunch in a riverside pub in Greenwich, the Trafalgar Tavern, then walked and sat in Greenwich Park. Every detail of the operation was talked through. Questions were asked, suggestions made, all points discussed. Only when all four were satisfied, and understood fully what they had to do, did they disperse. It had taken all afternoon.

Unknown to the team, because they didn't need to know, Rod drove to the home of a man he'd known as a boy at school. This boy had done a serious crime and Rod hadn't squealed on him. Joking around, the boy had started a fire in which an old woman had died trapped in her apartment. It was never solved, and the police still had it on their books as arson. It was a secret between Rod and Philip Turner, now a respected bank worker at Hounslow in West London. But there was another reason Rod paid this visit. Philip had served in the Royal Artillery before bad feet and persistent acne caused his discharge. But he knew the rudiments of gunnery, and that was his value to the operation.

Philip wasn't pleased to see Rod, and was horrified to hear what Rod wanted of him.

Rod insisted mercilessly, "There's a thousand in cash for you now, and my continued silence. Not bad for five minutes' work."

Philip still demurred; he couldn't do it; his nerve would go.

Rod raised his voice, "If I turn you in, it would kill your mother, wouldn't it?"

Philip hissed, terrified, "Sssh! She'll hear you, she's only in the next room."

It would indeed kill Mrs. Turner. Her Philip was her idol. Her only son and unmarried, they lived together and always would. How proud she was of him, now Chief Clerk in a small bank after twenty years of time serving; and secretary of the local Lions Club after years of trying and because no one else wanted the tiresome paperwok.

With extreme reluctance Philip eventually gave way under the threat of his past, pocketed the £1,000 in cash, and took in the simple instructions. Rod made him repeat them twice.

Then from his briefcase Rod took out a mobile phone, "You will use this. The number to call is taped on the back so you can't lose it. When you've done, throw the phone into a pond or river. Don't keep it. Is that clear?"

Wide-eyed, Philip nodded. Rod said menacingly, "Fail in this, and you're done for." Philip had no doubt that Rod meant exactly what he said.

The next day Rod took the rigid raider round the coast and up the Thames. Running empty except for her fuel, she planed along smoothly at high speed under the thrust of the two powerful outboards. In the river itself he was careful to keep the speed down to avoid drawing attention. Passing the Thames Barrier he locked into the Greenland Dock yacht basin on the south bank in Limehouse Reach. All the equipment, minus the explosives, was in a rented lock-up garage in Rope Street nearby. The explosives and weapons were still on the Theseus.

The young lads who hung about in a gang around Tabard Gardens at Bermondsey in south London thought it was Christmas come early. Here was this rich old guy who was crazy enough to give them loads of fireworks for free, so long as they didn't set them off till midnight on Saturday, and there was ten pounds apiece if they'd stick exactly to what he said. It was his wife's birthday, see, and she loved fireworks, so it was a surprise treat for her. They'd both be standing by Tower Pier at midnight, and to make sure it was exactly midnight when they started setting them off. Spike was their leader, and there was twenty five pounds in it for him if he could make sure they did it right, and from the green space exactly opposite Tower Pier. Rod made a show of giving Spike the twenty five.

Spike said with evident swagger, "That'll be no problem, guv, 'cos I'll bleedin' do 'em if they gimme any lip."

The large brown boxes of fireworks were handed over, and Spike's minions carted them into a small shed round the back of Staple Street.

Three days to go and Mac joined Rod on the Theseus. They locked out of St. Katherine's Dock and headed off downriver for the day. "To get the cobwebs out of her", they had said.

Passing Greenland Dock, Mike and Bill brought the raider out and followed at a discreet distance. It was a week-day, and well out in the estuary, away from the shipping lanes, they were undisturbed. With an angle grinder they cut the end caps off the booms, and the heavy shells were loaded carefully into the raider. The propellant charges followed, then the fuses and the weapons from the oil drums. The empty drums were hacked with an axe and held under till they sank. The booms were cut free and heaved over the side. The stern gantry stayed in place; it would change the boat's appearance too much to remove it. The contents of the raider, now well laden, were covered with tarpaulin. Arranged flat in the bottom, the cargo didn't look too bulky or conspicuous.

Going back upriver with the flood tide, Mac took the helm on the Theseus, with Bill as his crew, and they locked back into their berth in St. Katherine's Dock. The raider peeled off in Limehouse reach, and tied up briefly under the tall piles of the West India Dock pier. In the deep shadows of this massive structure, Rod climbed into his diving equipment and slid over the side. With him he carried a steel mesh sack clipped to his waist.

It wasn't a long swim, more of a drift with the tide doing all the work. Hugging the northern bank, the few times he put his head up for sightings were so brief, and exposed so little of his head, that the short lop common in the Thames hid him completely. Wapping Dock Stairs he glimpsed very briefly, then drifted under Wapping Pier. Another hundred yards, and taking great care, he located the smooth downstream pile of the Wapping Police Station pontoon. Moored to this were two or three police launches. It was, after all, the Headquarters of the Thames Division, Metropolitan Police.

Tying himself to the pile, well below the surface, Rod paid out the dark blue rope slowly until he was central under the big pontoon. Massively built of steel, it was the floating diesel fuel bunker for the police patrol boats. Looking up he could see and hear the screws turning as the boats pulled in and away on their routine patrols.

The undersea oil exploration business has had some useful spin-offs, and one of them was a powerful adhesive which sets on contact with sea water. Working slowly, and with great care to avoid making any sound, Rod used a chisel to scrape away weed, slime and paint till he got down to the bare metal. He let the chisel drop to the river bed. From his waist bag he took in turn three steel plates, each with a stout ring welded on. Coating each liberally with adhesive squeezed from a big tube, he pressed each plate firmly into place and held it there. The plates were fixed in a triangle pattern, about a yard apart. It took twenty minutes before he was satisfied with the hold of the plates. Gripping each ring in turn, he put his feet on the pontoon and pulled with all his strength. They were rock solid. Nothing was going to shift them.

Pulling himself along the rope to the mooring pile, he undid the rope, stowed it carefully, and drifted away upstream, being careful not to surface as he was now lighter by the weight of the plates and some tools. Taking a bearing from his wrist compass, and timing one hundred yards, he swam steadily due south underwater. He hadn't lost his touch. He saw the loom of the Cherry Garden pier on Bermondsey Wall and sought the heavy shadows beneath it. He had calculated his drift to within thirty yards. Not bad.

A quick glance showed Mike approaching slowly downstream in the raider. It seemed to pause briefly below the pier, and in that instant Rod was over the side and under the tarpaulin. The boat continued slowly downstream as Rod wriggled out of his diving equipment and dressed again normally. They locked back into Greenland Dock and tied up at their berth. Satisfied with the anonymous look of the raider, they both left. They daren't attempt a transfer of the explosives to the lock-up garage. It would be too risky. They would just have to take their chances on snoopers poking about.

The Commissioner of the Metropolitan Police, Sir Edward Morton, hated State Visits, and so did most of his colleagues.

Frankly, as he put it, they were, "A pain in the ass."

The crime figures always went up because the criminals knew perfectly well that a large part of the Met would be on royal route protection duties, traffic direction, crowd control, and the myriad other tasks which tied them up. And this time, worse luck, it was a week-end, and a summer one at that. London was jammed with tourists.

All the police Divisional Heads were at the morning conference as they went through their well practiced routine. Each detailed their measures taken, staff deployed, and so on. Special Branch had not detected any particular threat this time, and the visit of the King and Queen of Thailand had gone without incident. F4 Division had Ireland on it's mind as usual, but there seemed to be a summer lull in Irish activities. F4 Intelligence had nothing from their informers of anything special being planned by demonstrators or hot-heads. Thames Division had no particular worries; there was the usual summer increase in the number of 'floaters', drunks drowning after falling in. It was a pity though that because the Division was not involved directly in the forthcoming State Visit that so many of it's personnel had been taken for duties elsewhere. It left them very thin on the water, and would cut their patrol activities by half over that week-end.

The Commissioner summed up and thanked them for attending, "Let's make this one incident free, gentlemen. Her Majesty goes to Balmoral next week, and I know the whole force could do with a break. As for me, my good lady and I are off to the Italian Dolomites, and no, I'm not leaving a phone number."

The audience had the good sense to chuckle politely at 'Sir's' attempt at humor, and filed out. He had expressed all their thoughts. They'd had enough and were worn down by the pressures of their work. It had been a hot summer, and it was forecast to be a cloudy week-end with occasional light rain.

On the morning of Friday 25th July, Major General Arthur Geoffrey Gordon Meadows CB, CBE, reached his desk at the usual time and began to open his mail. He preferred to do it himself. He didn't like his staff reading his private correspondence.

He enjoyed his title and his work, so-called: Resident Governor of Her Majesty's Palace and Fortress, The Tower of London. He was lucky to be there. As his decorations showed, he was not a distinguished soldier. At no time had his career taken him into active service. But it was a career completely 'by the book'; there had been no blunders of any sort. It was his luck to have been at

Gordonstoun School, as had Prince Phillip and Prince Charles, and the Palace had chosen Meadows as a young Major to be an Equerry to the Royal Household.

Meadows was a good horseman, fitted in well at the many social functions, and above all was discreet. He never breathed a word of the several affairs he witnessed on the royal yacht Britannia or elsewhere. His eventual reward had been the grace and favor appointment to the Governorship of the Tower of London. He would never get his 'K', his Knighthood, which was a bitter disappointment to Lucy, his social climbing wife. She wanted above all to be Lady Meadows.

The General's mail that Friday morning looked routine except for one high quality vellum envelope, unstamped. He opened it carefully and smiled with pleasure as he read it. Embossed in maroon across the top was that most powerful of logos, Buckingham Palace.

'Dear General Meadows,

Her Majesty is graciously pleased to require your presence to join her and the President of Egypt at the State Apartments, Windsor Castle, on the evening of Saturday 26th July, 11 p.m.

The President has expressed an interest in the Tower of London and it's history, and Her Majesty feels that your presence would be helpful.

The late hour is regretted, but you will appreciate that the State Banquet will not end till perhaps 10 p.m, and Her Majesty will need to retire before joining her guests in the State Apartments. Please wait in your car by the West Gate from 11 p.m. and an Equerry will be sent to conduct you into the presence as soon as Her Majesty can receive you.

As this is a personal invitation, it has not been relayed through the Chief of Staff, and we would be grateful if you would inform no one else.

Yours sincerely,

Sir Nigel Cavendish

Private Secretary.'

A warm glow of pride permeated the General. No, he wouldn't tell Lucy till afterwards; she couldn't keep it to herself; she'd have to brag about it to her female cronies. She would press him, but he would say it was a late invitation to a military dinner, and she knew how late they went on once old comrades began to reminisce.

After the Commissioner's conference, a police car dropped the Chief Superintendent of Thames Division back to his Headquarters at Wapping. He pressed the correct code into the key-pad at the side entrance to the building and went in. There was a good view of the river even from there. He walked up the stairs to his office to be greeted by his secretary.

"Anything special in the mail?", he asked.

"No, Sir, except for this one; it's marked Personal and Private and looks a bit classy. Came by courier half an hour ago."

Chief Superintendent Ronald Playford sat in his swivel chair, and by habit spun round till he was facing the superb view of the river from his window. He never tired of it; there was always something moving in the way of shipping. He regretted that in two years' time retirement would be on him. He loved the river and anything to do with it. At one time he had thought of a career beyond Chief Superintendent, but had consciously chosen to stay in Thames Division knowing it was a minority branch from which few stars were born. The hotshots chose F3 Division, International and Serious Crime; or F4 Division, Prevention of Terrorism; or F6 Division, Security and Intelligence Services. From 1995 the rank of Chief Superintendent had been abolished, but those who held it at that time were still addressed by it. 'Old Ron's' people still called him by it. He was touchy about it.

From force of habit he fingered the pale cream envelope and inspected both sides. No paper clips or staples inside. He slit the letter carefully with the silver-plated paper knife his daughter had given him for a 25th anniversary present.

He read the letter slowly, then swore, "Bugger! My mess kit is at the cleaners!"

He phoned home and with much emphatic persuasion convinced his wife that she must retrieve his dress uniform today and not Monday as she had planned; yes, even though it meant a special trip.

He re-read the letter. It differed in some details from the General's.

'Dear Chief Superintendent Playford,

Her Majesty is graciously pleased to require your presence to join her and the President of Egypt at the State Apartments, Windsor Castle, on the evening of Saturday 26th July at 11 p.m.

The President has expressed an interest in the workings of the Thames River Police, it's long history and operations. He feels that perhaps the Cairo River Police might benefit from our long experience in these matters, and suggests the possibility of a visit there by you in an advisory capacity. Her Majesty feels therefore that your presence to discuss these matters would be helpful.

The late hour is regretted, but you will appreciate that the State Banquet will not end till perhaps 10 p.m, and Her Majesty will need to retire before joining her guests in the State Apartments. Please wait in your car by the West Gate from 11 p.m , and an Equerry will be sent to conduct you into the presence as soon as Her Majesty can receive you.

As this is a personal invitation it has not been relayed through the Commissioner, but he would be informed in due course should your presence in Egypt be requested.

Meanwhile we rely on your discretion to inform no one of this invitation.

Yours sincerely,
Sir Nigel Cavendish
Private Secretary   Mess Dress.'

Well, it would certainly be interesting; and a stay in Cairo; hey, that would be a great highlight on which to end. But his mind was mainly on what he should say. How was he supposed to address all these high-flown people? He decided he would call them all 'Sir' and be done with it.

What his mind was very much not concerned with was the fact that the Tower of London came under his jurisdiction at Wapping Police Station as the first point of reference for assistance in any emergency, and that it was a mile away via a slow and complex road system.

At mid-morning on Saturday 26th July, Rod collected the white BMW from the South London garage and drove to the retirement home near the river. Working out from there, he drove round in slowly widening arcs till he found what he wanted, a woman traffic warden. She was middle aged, overweight, hot, and looked like her feet hurt from pounding the pavement.

He slowed, lowered his window, and shouted loudly, "Piss off, you silly fat old bitch!", and drove slowly away towards the retirement home.

'Silly' she could stand; even 'old bitch'; she'd been called worse. It was the 'fat' which got to her. She was very touchy about her paunchy midriff and spreading hips, specially as she was trying so hard with her diet.

Through tight lips she spat out, "White BMW, I'll have you, you bastard if I ever come across you again!", and she changed her route to go in the direction the car had gone.

Rod drove to the retirement home and parked on the double yellow lines, with two wheels up on the kerb. This gave him room to get underneath. Wearing gloves and goggles against the rust, with a cordless drill he put numerous large holes in the full exhaust run and mufflers. He packed his kit in a small satchel and walked away. The keys he hid on top of the left rear wheel.

An hour later she found it, "Ah! So there is some justice after all. Double yellows and a kerb. See how you feel about this, you bastard!"

Rarely had she slammed a ticket on a windscreen with such relish. Her day had improved a whole lot.

In the Scotland Yard office of Raymond Scopes, duty Deputy Commissioner, Metropolitan Police, the intercom buzzed,

"Commander Farrant here, Sir, F4. We've got a threat notice on the State Visit which I think you ought to see."

"Right, bring it up."

Farrant arrived, and without touching the paper, slid a note from a folder onto Scopes' desk. Scopes aligned the note with a pencil. It was on cheap paper, in ball-point pen, clumsily written.

He read it out loud, "We the righteous people of Egypt who serve the Will of Allah, will bring our nation back to the true path of Islam and end degenerate Western habits. Our President must learn that our power cannot be stopped. We will today attack London Airport from the air.

The Muslim Brotherhood."

Scopes added calmly, "Brief me, Commander."

"Came in half an hour ago, post-marked Central London; no prints except our girl who scanned it then opened it. The Muslim Brotherhood are real and they have a tough track record. They've used bombs in Egypt to kill tourists."

"Yes, I've heard of them", said Scopes, "But London Airport from the air? Could they do it?"

"Unlikely, Sir, but not impossible. These boys are into suicide, so a light aircraft packed with explosives could be crashed into a terminal or a row of aircraft. It would make a hell of a mess."

Scopes paused only briefly, "Yes, we can't ignore this. I'll have to call in the Commissioner. He won't like it, he's playing golf. Send a car for him at once, Farrant, and a senior man to brief him on the way in. Get him on his mobile and tell him the car is on the way."

"Right, Sir."

As Farrant left, the intercom buzzed again. Scopes' secretary spoke, "Ten Downing Street on the line, Sir, the P.M's Private Secretary."

"Put him through."

"Good morning, Deputy Commissioner, I understand the Commissioner is not present at this time. We have a note here from some people calling themselves the Muslim Brotherhood. I'm sending it round to you now by car. Let us know your assessment in due course, will you?"

"Thank you, Sir, we appear to have the same note. I've called in the Commissioner and we'll report to you as soon as we can."

Within minutes a third note was reported from the Daily Mirror newspaper and was on it's way by taxi.

Scopes spoke curtly into his intercom, "Find the Chief of the Air Staff and get him here as soon as possible. Ask him to bring an aide with him. Use the authority of the Commissioner if you have to, and say we have a serious aerial threat in prospect. Then call an immediate conference of all the senior people in the building down to Commander, and I mean all. Get moving."

As luck would have it, the Chief of the Air Staff, Air Marshal Sir Frederick Miles, was about to leave home by helicopter for an air show; instead it could get him to the conference in half an hour.

The meeting assembled and Scopes began to brief it, using an overhead projector to display the three notes. They were virtually identical, certainly written by the same person. Inputs were invited from all who chose to make them. The Commissioner and the Air Marshal arrived almost simultaneously.

They listened to Scopes' summary, then the Commissioner spoke, "Thank you, Deputy Commissioner. These people are known terrorists. We must take them seriously. Air Marshal, please tell us what you think can be done."

The Air Marshal seemed young for his rank, and wore the ribbons of a distinguished flying career. His quiet delivery carried conviction.

"It's a complex problem. We must assume it's a light aircraft. If flown very low, and I mean roof-top height, their radar signature is very small indeed, and almost undetectable because of ground clutter."

He looked round the audience, "You might recall the light aircraft which landed in Red Square in Moscow in broad daylight after flying through the full might of their air defenses. At night and without lights the problem is even worse. We can mount standing air patrols, but we can't join civilian air traffic with any safety ; we'd have to stand off at a distance and rely on dash speed to make an interception."

He looked grim as he ended, "Once in contact we couldn't use missiles amongst other aircraft, we'd have to use cannon fire, and I must warn you that cannon shells fired across an airport or housing would have a devastating effect, certainly causing fires and probable loss of life."

There was a long silence, then the Commissioner spoke, "Thank you, Air Marshal. Our choices are simple, to act or not to act. The latter can't be an option in view of these people's track record. Therefore we must act accordingly."

Turning to the Air Marshal, he said, "Please set up standing air patrols as soon as you can. I will get confirmation passed to you via the Secretary of Defense that you have the authority to open fire. I will have all flying clubs monitored by their local police forces so no aircraft takes off without being checked by us. What I can't do is to check all those small fields around the country from which a light aircraft can fly. We'll have to take a chance on that. And thank you, Air Marshal, you have much to do; I'll keep you informed of any further developments."

The Air Marshal and his aide rose and left. The Commissioner fired off a series of orders. These amounted in total to a heavy concentration of police presence towards London Airport on the western outskirts of the city.

He ended with, "I'll speak now to the Airport, The Prime Minister, and Buckingham Palace, in that order. Keep me informed at all times please", and he swept out of the room.

The whole of Rod's raiding team had been working on their alibis. Mac was at home in his pub in Suffolk, 'feeling not too well, and upstairs in bed'. Molly would call out to him from time to time so customers could hear. Bill and Mike had each 'gone to see the late show' at their local cinemas, then home. Rod made them see the films the night before so they would be word perfect on the stories.

Rod had a drink in the Dickens Bar at St. Katherine's Dock at lunchtime with his good friend from the luxurious cruiser, the Galatea. Rod explained he wanted to give a party for his many good friends in the yacht harbor, but the Theseus was far too small, and he had several cases of good champagne waiting to be consumed. Sure, he was welcome to the Galatea for the night, and what a good idea; let's make it a party to remember. Memorable it was certainly going to be.

So it was by 10 p.m. on the night of Saturday 26th July, that Rod was very firmly fixed in the minds of all the men and glamorous girls on board the Galatea that he was a convivial and generous host, a damn good laugh, and the life and soul of the party.

CHAPTER 5: ATTACK

The Tower of London in theory could have up to 150 people living there. In practice it was never that number. There should have been about forty Yeoman Warders or Beefeaters and their families. It was a condition of their job that they had to be retired Warrant Officers from the Army, Royal Marines or Air Force who had served at least twenty two years. Most had served all their active lives. This made them all old men. In fact, through deaths and retirements through ill health, Rod knew the number of Yeoman Warders was well below strength. He had seen the advertisements asking for applicants. The Governor had a staff of three, and a Chaplain. The personnel were to a man and woman well into their sixties. Their job was entirely ceremonial. They were not a fighting force, nor equipped to deal with one.

The nightly Tower Guard might be a different proposition though. One junior Officer, one Sergeant, and twelve soldiers from the regiment on London ceremonial duties formed each night's guard. At 9 p.m. they paraded in full dress uniform for the 900 year old Ceremony of the Keys. The old guard went off duty and the new guard came on. The Officer had his own room; the Sergeant and the men their own guardroom where they brewed tea, played cards or watched television while half the guard patrolled the grounds. There was a single sentry box at the entrance to the Jewel House. No one seriously expected an attempt on the jewels. There hadn't been one since 1671, and that had failed. It was known to be impossible. There were too many electronic defenses. The vaults had thick steel walls and doors, the best that Britain's safe makers could devise. The guards' real duty was to stop the occasional drunks and jokers who tried to climb in for a bet or to impress their girls.

The guards carried rifles, the clumsy and unreliable 5.56 mm, but the optical sights were so prone to damage they were always covered. Each man carried the short knife bayonet, but not on his rifle, always in it's scabbard. None carried any ammunition, and it had never been issued. It was stored in the guardroom and had to be fetched from there if required. It was one of the Sergeant's duties to check it and sign for it. No way was any British Guards Regiment Sergeant going to risk losing rounds and having to explain away such sloppiness to his superiors. None of the young men there that Saturday night wanted to be there. They'd rather be down at the disco with their friends, trying to charm the girls, and with luck, getting laid.

Very few cars resided in the Tower grounds; there wasn't room for them. The Governor, by his right of office, could keep his car there. That evening before the Keys Ceremony he told the Chief Yeoman Warder that his car would leave by the usual exit at 10 p.m. and not return till after midnight. The gates between the Lanthorn Tower and Salt Tower, and between the Cradle Tower and Well Tower, were to be single locked and not barred, and the Guard Commander informed. This was duly done, to the young Officer's disappointment. The usual glass of Port or two in the Governor's residence would have to be missed. A pity because it alleviated the dull duty. At 10 p.m. the Governor's car left. He knew the meaning of military punctuality. No summer traffic problems would delay his long drive right across London, nor his arrival at Windsor and the pleasurable late evening he anticipated so much.

Mac, Bill and Mike had quietly loaded the raider from the lock-up garage, and moved out onto the river before the yacht basin shut for the night. They picked up a mooring in deep shadow and waited. Each knew the exact layout of the Tower by heart. They had studied the plans Rod gave them. None of these plans remained at home. All had been destroyed. As darkness fell, Mac rigged a small alloy mast on the bow of the raider. It showed the regulation white, green and red lights needed for night movement on the river. No police patrol boat was going to pick them up for some minor lighting infringement.

At 11 p.m. precisely they cast off and picked up Rod from St. George's Stairs on the south bank. He had run over Tower Bridge to join them.

Rod's final briefing was short, "OK, just remember about the goods and what I've told you. We need very few pieces, only the crowns and scepters. You've all studied the pictures, but there'll be a lot of smoke and damage about, so we must keep looking till we get what we need. When we get 'em we're out and away."

Then with a smile at the team, "And don't go stealing other stuff. Yes, I know it will be tempting, but don't do it, it's too risky. Anyway, if you come across bits like the Grand Punch Bowl it's nearly a quarter of a ton in solid gold and you'd get ruptured trying to lift it."

They chuckled appreciatively. They all felt good about the operation. It was good to be in action again, good to be on the way to getting rich. They all trusted Rod; they'd served under him before; they knew he could make it work; they wouldn't be there if they didn't think that. Marines had that kind of personal loyalty and trust. Within the Special Boat Service it was doubly strong.

Rod looked at his watch, "Right, let's do it!" The raider began to purr quietly upstream towards Tower Bridge.

At the Royal Air Force base at Coltishall in Norfolk two more Tornado fighter aircraft roared down the runway on full afterburners and climbed away towards London.

As they turned, Squadron Leader Williams said acidly into his radio, "This is a bloody waste of time. Third trip today and nothing's happened. Still, we're getting the hours in."

The duty air traffic controller replied calmly, "Radio silence please, Tango One.", and thought he heard a faint, "Up yours", before the planes disappeared.

To say that Philip Turner was nervous that night would be to put it mildly. His mother couldn't understand why he had to go out so late and leave her all alone. She might be murdered in her bed. He said it was a special collection for the Lions, and he wouldn't be long. The mobile phone he had wiped clean, and wearing gloves he put it in a plastic shopping bag and got into his rusty small Ford car. He drove to the airport and parked properly in the short stay area.

Terminal Two was called the Queen's Building because she had opened it. There was a spectator viewing area on the roof where aircraft buffs gathered during the day, but it closed an hour before dusk. Below it, inside the building, was still the best view out over the airport, though slightly restricted by pillars in the structure.

There weren't many people about. The airport was in the West London suburbs, so noise regulations prevented flying after midnight, though delayed aircraft did sometimes land later.

Philip was early, he always was. He bought a hot chocolate drink and sipped it slowly. Tea and coffee made him jumpy. He looked at his watch every few seconds and nervously eyed the bag with the phone it.

At Windsor Castle well before 11 p.m, Major General Meadows' car drew up in the sloping drive outside the West Gate. He could see clearly the royal flag floodlit atop the main tower indicating the Queen was in residence. He switched on his interior light and began to re-read his notes on the history of the Tower of London, although he knew them already.

The sentry on guard duty in the box by the gate didn't move a muscle, just his eyes swiveled. Unless he was mistaken, that was a General in full mess kit. He would go and have a look. With a crash of steel-studded boots he snapped to attention, shouldered his rifle, made a smart turn and paced steadily across the gateway. He slammed to a halt by the car's door and smacked the butt of his rifle

68

in a smart salute. The General nodded in acknowledgement, and the sentry turned and resumed his place. The General's sense of pleasurable anticipation heightened.

Chief Superintendent Playford's wife had made him wear a sports jacket for the drive to Windsor, "You'll crease your uniform jacket, dear", she said as she fussed over him.

His car arrived at 10.55 and he pulled up behind the General. Playford could see a senior military officer in bright scarlet mess kit was also waiting to go in. It was reassuring to know he wouldn't be alone with that lot.

The policeman on West Gate duty saw the General park and thought little of it. A whole convoy of official cars had gone in earlier, some under police escort. But this second car which had just arrived appeared to contain a civilian. He would go and check on it. Five yards away the driver got out, doffed the sports jacket and donned the tunic and cap of a Chief Superintendent.

The policeman saluted, "Evening, Sir."

"Good evening, Constable, I'm waiting to go in."

"Yessir, it's been a busy evening", and he turned and resumed his patrol.

At about 11.30 the West Gate opened and several cars came out in convoy. Their lights dazzled so the General and Playford couldn't make out the occupants. Won't be long now, thought the General; the minor guests are leaving. Soon the Equerry would appear to conduct him into Her Majesty's gracious presence. It was well worth the wait.

With Rod steering, the raider trickled slowly under Tower Bridge. As it reappeared on the other side it's lights were out. On tickover it was barely audible. The high tide was almost at it's peak and about to turn. It was raining very lightly as the retired Royal Navy cruiser, HMS Belfast, loomed up on the left like a giant gray steel monster. The landing stage fixed to her starboard side was for the ferry across to Tower Pier. Rod and Mike padded silently up the walkway to Belfast's main deck and crouched low, listening.

The night guard on HMS Belfast was two men from the Force 4 security firm. Their base in the ship was the Walrus Café, forward on the port side. One guard patrolled while the other drank tea and watched TV. They made their rounds in turn. In light rain the one on a circuit would be in shelter somewhere. Rod moved quietly forward as Mike moved aft. Mike found the guard smoking under an overhang on the boat deck. Mike felled him with one blow, taped his mouth, and handcuffed him to a stanchion.

Finding Rod again, they followed the signs kindly provided for the tourists and came to the door of the brightly lit Walrus Café. Music came from inside. Rod and Mike were in the door and floored the guard before he could move. He was taped and cuffed to a table.

Back on deck, Rod and Mike ran to the gangway and signaled OK. Bill ran up with insulated bolt cutters, across to the port quarter, and cut the main shore power line to the ship. The Belfast fell into darkness. It might be noticed from the shore, but only as an electrical fault that would be fixed next day. No problem.

On the grassy space near the Belfast about a dozen scruffy youths gathered round several big cardboard boxes.

It had stopped raining but the lads were impatient, "Aw, come on, Spike, let's light the friggin' things and piss off; I'm fed up waiting."

Spike was adamant, "Nah, the old guy said twelve, and twelve it's gonna be. You wanna argue?"

The smaller lad shook his head and looked at his watch.

On the ship the heavy shells came up the gangplank first. They weighed 115 lbs each and could just be lifted and carried. The team had been training with this weight for the past weeks. Getting the shells up to B Turret, the highest one, was hard work, but sweating in their black rubber suits, all the equipment was at last in place. Inside the darkened B Turret each now donned a head lamp wired to a battery pack at the waist.

Rod said quietly, "Now comes the tough bit."

Each turret weighed 135 tons, but was designed for manual operation if the ship's power failed. Both forward turrets were still capable of operation because they were rotated to starboard and the guns elevated to about 45 degrees.

As the sign told the tourists, 'The guns in both turrets are trained and elevated onto a target some 20 kilometers away outside North West London, the Scratchwood Services Area on the M1 Motorway, a reminder of the awesome power of naval gunnery.'

The government was about to get such an awesome demonstration.

Mac had served on the Belfast as a young Marine and he knew the drills exactly. The Marines on board Royal Navy warships always manned X Turret. There was intense competition between the Marines and Navy gun crews to be the most efficient and rapid into action.

He handed out cans of aerosol freeing-up oil, "Spray this all round the rack and pinions!"

Two huge handles from the turret walls were inserted into their sockets. It was a four man job, two per handle, to move the turret. Locking pawls knocked free with a hammer, they sweated on the handles, full weight and strength. It looked hopeless at first, four men to move 135 tons. But the aerosol oil got through to the big roller bearings, and millimeter slowly the big turret began to creep round. Once moving, two men could keep it going.

"Stop at 264 degrees", ordered Rod.

Mac watched the scale, "264 on."

"Depress port gun to horizontal", said Rod.

Mac spun the handwheel till the huge breech rose up level.

"Load!", ordered Rod firmly but calmly.

Mac unlocked the big quarter-threaded breech block and swung it open. Mike and Bill heaved a heavy shell into the loading tray , and checked the base fuse was screwed home. Then both on a wooden rammer they slammed the shell hard up into the chamber, so the copper driving band seated properly in the barrel's rifling. Next followed the big propellant charge with it's igniter. Mac swung the breech shut and rotated it into the locked position.

"Elevate to 48 degrees", said Rod.

Mac spun the wheel again and the breech dropped quickly, "48 on!"

Rod said, "Standby!"

He stepped outside the turret and took out his mobile phone. He punched in some numbers.

Philip Turner nearly died of fright when the phone in his shopping bag began to bleep. He fumbled for it hurriedly and put it to his ear.

He heard the single command, "Standby!"

He walked across to the full length windows and stood looking out across the airport. All he could see was a myriad of runway and perimeter lights, and several parked aircraft being unloaded or refueled. His hands shook.

High above and ten miles to the east, Tango One eased his buttocks on the hard parachute pack in his Martin Baker ejector seat, and spoke into the boom mike on his helmet.

He was not a happy man, "Tango One to Coltishall control. Midnight now, nothing happening. Looking down at solid overcast and a cloudbase of 1,000 feet. Request permission to break off."

"Wait, Tango One", a pause, then, "Affirmative, return to base, flight level three five, use runway zero two."

"Affirmative, Coltishall control, breaking off now", followed by a muttered, "Thank God for that!"

Squadron Leader Williams swung the stick over and pressed on the rudder bar to make a neat turn which his Number Two could follow.

At Windsor, Chief Superintendent Playford had had enough. He'd waited nearly an hour and he was angry. He knew the royals were a law unto themselves, but this was bloody rude. He got out of his car, slammed the door, and walked down the West Approach to find a duty policeman. Police Constable James was unpleasantly surprised to find an irate Chief Superintendent bearing down on him.

Playford snapped, "Get through to your controller and say a Chief Superintendent and an Army General are waiting outside the West Gate of Windsor Castle, by invitation, and we would like to speak to someone on the castle staff."

P.C. James did this and got an acknowledgement. Five minutes later a small door opened in the main gate and an official emerged. The two invitation letters were inspected.

The official was apologetic, "I'm very sorry, gentlemen, there appears to have been some mistake. Her Majesty retired to bed half an hour ago after her guests left. Please take this up with the Palace tomorrow."

"I most certainly will!", snorted the General.

Playford didn't wait, he gunned his car down the drive, muttering angrily, "What bastard on the force would pull a trick like that? I bet it's that sod Robinson. He's been out for a laugh at my expense. He'll spread it all round the Division."

And so it was that at midnight the Commanding Officer of the Tower of London, and the Chief Officer of the Police Headquarters charged with guarding it, were both in their cars ten miles away and heading into the late night traffic in West London.

Beside the Belfast, Spike yelled, "OK lads, light 'em up and watch 'em go!"

73

"Yeah, I'll have some of that!", piped a little helper, and they set about lighting the extensive array of fireworks they had covered with pieces of plastic sheeting. The rain had stopped, and rockets and maroons began to storm into the sky with repeated loud explosions.

Rod put his head through the turret door and shouted, "Shoot!"

The huge naval gun went off with a deafening roar as the breech recoiled back into the turret.

Spike swore, "Bloody 'ell! What was that?"

"One of the ship's guns went off, I fink", said an excited little youth.

"Cor! Brilliant! What a friggin' show!", yelled Spike.

The Belfast rocked slightly as the huge shell sped on it's high, curving flight lasting over half a minute. London Airport was a massive 3,000 acres in area, and Rod had aimed for the far side of it, away from the Terminals. There was a heavy crump as the shell landed and buried itself fifty feet in the ground. The delayed-action fuse took one eleventh of a second to function, the same as a blink, before with an enormous roar and a gout of flame a hundred foot high column of dirt and smoke shot into the air. The Terminals shook with the shock waves. The shell had landed just in from the Western Perimeter Road near the Perry Oaks Sewage Works.

Philip Turner jerked with fright, but his training took over. He punched the buttons on his phone, "Left 400, down 400", and put the phone back in his bag.

Airport Security had stood down from it's top level of alert after midnight, assuming the Muslim Brotherhood notes to be a hoax. Now the junior and inexperienced Duty Officer frantically rang the Metropolitan Police Operations Room and began shouting down the phone, "Airport under attack! One heavy explosion on the far side of the Terminals, apparently from the air or by mortar, no casualties reported yet!"

On the ship, Mac had brought the gun barrel to horizontal and swung open the breech. Acrid fumes spilled out into the turret. With no fans running the smoke began to swirl about. With an ordinary dampened mop Mike swabbed out the gun's breech and chamber to remove any smoldering propellant, and a second shell was rammed home. The barrel was elevated and Mac put in the new settings.

"Shoot!", said Rod, and again the huge breech recoiled back into the turret.

Half a minute later the second shell hit the southern runway, penetrated completely through it and exploded, heaving giant concrete slabs high in the air and leaving a deep crater.

Philip Turner's nerve only just held. He wasn't going to risk a hit on a Terminal and possibly injure himself.

He called into the phone, "Left 100, down 500", and turned to walk away down the stairs.

He was in the main concourse when the third shell hit. It landed between two parked fuel tankers on the edge of the Cargo Area concrete apron. 10,000 gallons of aviation fuel went up in a fireball which could be seen for miles around. The explosions, plus the flames, convinced most people within a five mile radius that a major air crash had occurred.

The Airport Duty Officer was going berserk down the phone to the Metropolitan Police Operations Room, "Three heavy detonations! One runway hit, major fires close to the Cargo Terminal, casualties not known yet. Yes! From the air! Like the bloody warning said! It has to be aircraft or IRA mortar. If it's a mortar it's bloody huge! Radar reports nothing on their screens. Get a move on with your perimeter searches, we're sitting ducks here!"

Sirens wailed and people were running in panic from the Terminals towards the car parks. Turner's car was caught in the traffic jam, and he sat nervously waiting for it to clear. Eventually he crawled away onto the M4 motorway and drove home.

The Commissioner was woken at home and told the news. He swore and asked if the Prime Minister had been informed. He hadn't. "Right, I'll do it, and I'm coming in."

The Prime Minister had drunk too much again. He always did at big receptions. He often said the wrong thing too. This time he'd tried to amuse the President of Egypt's wife by reminding her that the cracks in the face of the Sphinx, so long studied by eminent archeologists, had in fact been caused by dynamiting in a quarry some distance away. A historian in her own right, she smiled glacially at the unintended insult to the incompetence of her countrymen. So the P.M. had taken too much Madeira, because he preferred it to the Port, and it was better than he had at 10 Downing Street. Now the insistent phone by his bed pulled him slowly awake.

He answered with a curt, "Yes?", and listened briefly, then said angrily, "Commissioner, what were the Air Force doing at this time? And what were the police patrols doing? I was under the distinct impression that all proper precautions had been taken."

"They had, Sir, but clearly were ineffective. I am investigating now and will report back when I have more details for you."

"Thank you, but not till morning please. I can't affect the outcome from here. You can imagine what the media are going to do with this, can't you? Good night." The P.M. replaced the phone, and with a groan rolled over and quickly fell back into a heavy stupor.

On the Belfast the big turret crept slowly round to the right till it was pointing at the Tower of London. With all three barrels horizontal and the breeches open, Rod inserted the dummy wooden shell he had made into the center barrel. It was, as planned, the perfect bore sight.

He called two orders, "Mike, we might have visitors soon; time to blow the shore gangplank", and, "Bill, take the flares out now and begin firing on my order."

Each left quickly and silently. Mike padded round to the port deck aft where the visitors' walkway came on board. Lying full length he pressed a small charge of plastic explosive under the walkway, pushed in a detonator and lit the short fuse. He slid back into the shadows and along the ship's side to B Turret. A bright flash accompanied the explosion which severed the walkway from the ship's side and it fell into the river with a heavy splash. The sound was lost among the exploding maroons and rockets still flashing up from Spike and his lads.

On the Galatea in St. Katherine's Dock three or four cabins had girls in with their legs spread wide, moaning as their mounts grunted and heaved into them. On deck more revelers stood watching the firework show clearly visible over the Tower Hotel.

"Now that's what I call a party!", mumbled one of them, fondling the breast of the girl propping him up.

Inside the Tower of London, the old gunners among the Yeomen Warders had woken to the first crash of the Belfast's guns. The three shells at London Airport had been fired in less than three minutes among the booming of Spike's rockets and mortars.

Retired Warrant Officer Walter Blackstone, Royal Artillery, swore under his breath. Doris his wife didn't like swearing. "Noisy sods! I could have sworn that was one of our old five point fives; sounded just like it."

Already seventy five feet high, B Turret had been raised a further twenty five feet by the high tide, and now stood 100 feet up. The Jewel House in the Waterloo Block would be in plain view.

Rod shouted, "Flares, go!", and Bill, kneeling on deck, held out the big Schermuly rocket flare at arm's length, twisted the base firing cap, and the rocket flashed to a height of 1,000 feet. The million candlepower brilliant white magnesium flare hung on it's parachute, drifting slowly towards the Tower in a slight breeze. An eerie glow lit up the underside of the low cloud-base.

Looking through the telescopic sight, Rod called swiftly for minor adjustments of the turret until the cross-hairs sat precisely in the center of the fourth window from the left at the base of the Waterloo Block. He pulled out the 'scope.

"Load!", he shouted, and three shells rammed home.

"Right, Mac, all three barrels on that setting. Shoot!"

The ship rocked as all three barrels fired at once and recoiled back into the turret. Working methodically the team loaded and fired nine more rounds in three salvos.

"Check, check, check!", shouted Rod, "We'll put the rest into the White Tower."

Mac spun the control wheels as Rod sighted down the 'scope in the center barrel till the guns were on the White Tower.

"Load and shoot!", yelled Rod and the remaining rounds crashed into the White Tower.

"Go!", yelled Rod.

It was the only signal they needed. At a run they boarded the raider and surged across the short distance to the Queen's Stairs. They had time to pull on gas masks over their hoods. The raider's alloy bows smashed onto the stone steps and rode half way up. The S.A.S, the Special Air Service, liked to interpret their initials as Speed, Aggression, Surprise. The Marines said their S.B.S, the Special Boat Service, stood for Speed, Boldness, Surprise. Here were four highly trained Marine Commandos doing what they knew best, and liking it.

Heaving packs onto their backs, the four all-black figures ran along the wharf at a low crouch and knelt by the wall at the base of the Cradle Tower. Sirens could be heard wailing in the distance, getting closer. Rod sprinted across to a bankside bench and pushed under it a sack containing three diving sets, then ran back again.

Rod Gave the order, "Go!", and Bill aimed a rocket grenade at the wooden gate between the Cradle Tower and Well Tower and fired. The gate disappeared in the explosion. The four of them were through and hidden inside the archway. Mike raised his rocket and fired. The second gate between the Lanthorn Tower and Salt Tower flew into fragments. Rod led the four into the interior.

A brief pause to check the scene revealed complete chaos, bells ringing, shouting, lights coming on in some of the buildings. Alarms had gone off as soon as the first shells struck the Waterloo Block. These alarms registered in the Headquarters, Thames Division, Metropolitan Police; New Scotland Yard Operations Room; the Duty Office, Army Headquarters, London Command, Knightsbridge Barracks; and the London Fire Service Headquarters. Each of these services reacted in their own way, and with widely varying response times, depending who was on duty after midnight on a Saturday.

Rod had chosen the best route into the interior of the Tower fortress. It had the most cover and allowed the most diversionary damage to be done. Moving at a low crouch, hugging the walls of the New Armories to the right, they threw phosphorus grenades through the unlit ground floor windows. Fires sprang up almost at once. To their left they threw smoke grenades. The smoke swirled round them covering their advance.

Flames belched out of the upper floors of the White Tower where the last shells had hit. They saw no one till level with the Constable Tower. A young sentry lurched out of the smoke and stopped dead when he saw the four black-suited and gas-masked men.

Rod shouted, "S.A.S! Where's the attack?"

The soldier yelled back, "Waterloo Block, Sir!", before Mac clubbed him to the ground. He was handcuffed behind his back, taped across the mouth, and thrown down in the shadow of the White Tower.

As Rod and the team crouched in the entrance to the Royal Fusiliers' Museum, their jumping off point for entry to the Jewel House, two men spotted them, a Yeoman Warder and the Sergeant of the Guard. He advanced at the run with a fixed bayonet. A baton round broke his shoulder and Mike clubbed him down. The Warder had more sense and put his hands up. Both were cuffed and taped and thrown behind the low Museum parapet wall.

The Waterloo Block containing the Jewel House had flames coming out of several windows at it's west end, but the main entrance was intact. A rocket grenade took out the door, and they were inside. Dumping all their kit in the entrance except what they needed, three of them turned left towards the jewels. Mike crouched on guard with a view out across the Broad Walk.

As Rod had planned, the shells from the Belfast had done their work. With their delayed-action fuses they had not detonated on impact with the outer walls, but as they were designed to do, had tunneled with immense force through the intervening structure like a hot knife through butter, and smashed into the steel wall of the vault.

The civilian safe-makers had no idea of the full power of heavy naval gunnery. Each massive armor-piercing hardened steel shell left their gun muzzles at 2,785 feet per second, and struck with a force of several hundred tons, focused onto the sharp pointed nose of each shell. Three of these had struck at once, only feet apart, delivering a blow of thousands of tons against the vault wall. Melting into the steel of the wall where they struck, the explosions of the three shells completed the work and cracked the vault wall. The following shells ripped into the weakened wall and tore a way in, filling the interior with white-hot chunks of flying steel.

Fires burned along their route through the Waterloo Block towards the Jewel House. Their headlamps lit the way as they wielded their CO_2 extinguishers and fought through the torn vault walls.

They had needed some luck and got it. Rod had gambled that the first salvo of three shells would hit the vault with such force that it would twist the whole structure and jam the mechanism for lowering the main regalia down into the vaults beneath. This had happened and the mechanism was jammed in the half lowered position.

Searching rapidly through the debris they began to find the items they needed and threw them into the sack Rod carried. He checked them off mentally as the flames grew fiercer and the smoke thicker.

"Come on! The Sovereign's Scepter!", he yelled.

Then Mac saw it jammed in the half lowered display platform. Using his crowbar, Mac levered aside a piece of twisted steel with his huge strength, and Bill reached down, picked out the scepter and shoved it in Rod's sack.

"That's it! Let's get out!", shouted Rod, and they needed no extra bidding. The short journey back to the entrance was a nightmare. The burning paneling split like rifle shots as it exploded in the flames. Using the last of their CO2 to clear a way they made it to the entrance and crouched down to gasp some cool air.

They re-donned their equipment as Mike said, "No intruders; people running about like headless chickens, even some women."

Rod took a small metal disc out of a belt pouch and dropped it in the doorway. Stamped crudely on the disc were the words, 'Remember 1916.'

Rod gave the command, "Right, you know the plan. Two smoke!", and two smoke grenades arced into the Broad Walk towards the White Tower. Through the dense smoke Rod led off towards the Constable Tower.

The sword thrust from the Guard Commander took Mac right through the thigh and he cursed in agony as he fell; Rod's blow broke the Officer's arm as Mike's fist smashed his jaw. He fell senseless.

Mac gritted, "Pull it out! Pull it out, you bastards!"

It took Rod a two-handed grip to withdraw the blade as Mac groaned from the intense pain. Rod held the blood-smeared sword clear of the ground for a good reason. They dragged Mac over to the Museum parapet and propped him against it.

"Field dressings!", ordered Rod, and two were applied and tied tightly in place, one to each wound from which the blood ran freely.

Rod said, "No arteries, you're lucky. Come on you old bastard, move!"

"Piss off!", muttered Mac as he heaved himself up.

"Take his kit", said Rod, and Mike and Bill relieved Mac of his load.

"Right, move down there forty yards", said Rod, "And keep this sword off the ground."

He went back to where the still senseless Guard Commander lay and pulled him across to the Museum parapet and put him behind it. Returning to the exact spot where Mac had fallen, Rod pulled the pin from a phosphorus grenade, put it on the ground and let the firing lever fly off. He sprinted towards the others as behind him the grenade exploded and the white heat of the phosphorus exposed to the air began to burn everything over a thirty yard radius.

They headed towards the Salt Tower at the best speed Mac could make. Their remaining smoke grenades gave more cover. Their last phosphorus grenades except one went into any rooms not on fire. They saw only one more person, a Yeoman Warder running towards them shouting for them to stop, and two baton rounds dropped him. Then they were out through the first gate and the second.

Flashing blue lights seemed to fill the sky and sirens wailed continuously. They donned the diving sets from under the bench.

Rod said, "OK, Mike, off you go", and Mike ran towards the raider. Just then a police launch appeared at high speed coming downstream from the Waterloo floating police station, and turned in towards the raider.

Rod ordered, "Rockets! But don't hit it!"

He shouldered his own and fired as Bill fired his. One rocket missed the bow by inches and exploded in the water, but the second struck the boat's extreme stern and blew off the transom, sinking the boat within thirty seconds. It's crew of three dived overboard and swam for their lives across the river.

Rod said, "Mac, are you sure you're up to the swim?"

"Sure, boss, I'm OK, a bit sore, but it's all down tide."

"OK, off you go."

Mac dropped into the water and disappeared. Bill followed at once. Rod threw the bloodstained sword as far out into the river as he could, then all the other kit after it. He waited briefly to see Mike safely away in the raider.

Once in the boat, Mike took the hand axe from it's clips and with two blows chopped big gashes in the exhaust runs of each engine, threw the axe in the river and started both motors. At full throttle he spun the craft and headed downstream. The exhaust gases which normally vented quietly underwater through the propeller hubs, now howled into the open air like two racing motorbikes. He spun the wheel to and fro making as much noise and wash as possible.

Rod glanced at his watch. The whole job, in and out, had taken less than ten minutes. He dropped into the water and sank like a stone to the bottom.

CHAPTER 6: ESCAPE

The guide books to the Tower of London were kind enough to publish the weights of each item in the Crown Jewels, and Rod knew exactly what weight he had in the nylon sack clipped to his waist. He sat on the riverbed, back to the tide and feet braced against it, and looked up as the propellers of two police launches churned overhead. Working mostly by feel, he took from a belt pouch a steel mesh sack made from three layers of braided stainless steel cable. With great care he pushed the nylon sack and it's priceless contents into the steel mesh one, and clipped it securely to his waist. He began to drop lead weights from his belt till he felt himself go light. Watching the loom of the lights through the water above him, he started to drift downstream.

Up above, Mike kept the raider's engines flat-out as he shot under Tower Bridge. Suddenly two police launches converged on him from downstream, catching him in their spotlights. He charged straight at them and at the last second they parted and the raider roared between them. They spun round in pursuit but he had twice their speed. Steadying the boat briefly, he unscrewed the caps from two full fuel cans and kicked them over, the gasoline swilling around the boat. Still screaming at full throttle the raider ran straight at St. George's Stairs. Twenty yards away Mike dropped the last phosphorus grenade into the fuel and did a backward roll off the boat. It hit the concrete steps and exploded in a huge fireball as Mike sank slowly downstream.

The explosion was the signal. Four young men in dark clothes picked up a sack each containing light metal scrap and ran away from the dockside shouting and laughing. A minute later they reached the white BMW, and still shouting and laughing loudly they threw their sacks in the trunk, slammed it hard, and slammed all four doors. Curtains twitched and lights came on in the retirement home as the sleepless and light sleepers peered out of their windows. With it's drilled exhaust and mufflers the engine roared like a racing car as the young driver gunned it. He let the clutch out with a bang and the wheels spun ferociously as the car accelerated away.

The old folks were unanimous in their disgust, "Well, really! Disgraceful! Hooligans! Ought to be a law against it!", and so on all the next morning.

At least ten angry residents of the Grove Street Retirement Home could give ten different descriptions of the getaway car and it's occupants.

The BMW's crew had orders to get noticed but not get booked, and they enjoyed every minute of it as they roared down to Dover, throwing the sacks into a field on the way. Boarding a ferry to France with their pre-paid tickets, they drank too much and boasted too much about their 'exploit'. In Calais they drove to the main railway station and left the car conspicuously in front of the main entrance, then walked to the nearby Hotel Bilancourt where their rooms were booked and paid for. Their cash was waiting in an envelope at the desk. The next day, as instructed, they came back by separate boats and enjoyed pre-paid first-class rail trips to London. It had been a good laugh, and good money with it, and if it screwed the cops, so much the better.

It was clear to the police, army and emergency services that they were dealing with a major terrorist attack against London Airport and the Tower of London. It was almost certainly the work of Irish dissidents known as the I.R.A, or Irish Republican Army. Only they could mount a twin attack on this scale and source the appropriate explosives. At the Tower, fire-fighting, damage control and attending to casualties was the immediate concern. The Waterloo Block was burning too fiercely to see what damage might have been done to the Jewel House. But the contents were bound to be safe, lowered away into their underground vault. It was impregnable, wasn't it. The I.R.A had done their work well. It would be a major media coup for them.

As Rod drifted downstream he hugged the north bank of the river, taking momentary sightings to check his position. He passed St. Katherine's Dock where the party on the Galatea became ever more drunken. Some of them had joined the crowds up on Tower Bridge Approach to gaze at the flames leaping up from the White Tower, but the police held the people back, and it started to rain again, so the Galatea continued to rock to the muted sounds of laughter down below. Rod passed Old Wapping Stairs and then the New Stairs and drifted cautiously towards the police station pontoon. Lights were ablaze in all the station's windows as shouting people ran down the walkway to board the patrol boats, held there expertly on the throttle by their helmsmen against the fast-flowing ebb tide.

With a final sighting, Rod bumped against the upstream mooring pile of the pontoon, well below the surface, and felt his way down it. He tied a loop of the dark rope around it, and began to pay it out slowly. It took two minutes of agonized groping before he felt the first of the three steel plates and rings and clipped himself securely to it. Pulling hard on each ring in turn, he re-checked their security. They were still rock solid. Using three strong steel cables through the mesh of the steel sack, he clipped each cable onto the rings using powerful stainless carabiners. He tested each in turn. Nothing was going to move those attachments. The steel mesh sack hung below the police pontoon, tugged lightly by the tide. In it were the chief Crown Jewels of the British Monarchy, impervious to the water flowing through them.

Now much lighter in weight, Rod had to use great care not to surface. He pulled himself downwards on his rope to the mooring pile. Gripping it with his legs, he undid the rope and stowed it, then released his grip. Swimming strongly now to stay submerged, he struck out downstream and added his own speed to that of the tide.

Mike and Bill made easy escapes. Both lived south of the river and had chosen to exit in Deptford Creek. They were well spaced in time as Mike's entry into the water was delayed by his evasion tactics in the raider. Bill swam slowly under Creek Road Bridge, and in it's black shadows dumped his kit in deep water. Swimming now only in a light undersuit, he climbed out on the Norman Road side of the creek, and quickly found his car in Tarves Way. The keys were hidden beneath it. He got in, changed quickly into dry clothes, and drove home. Mike arrived in the creek fifteen minutes later, followed the same pattern, but climbed out towards Creekside, picked up his car in Bronze Street and drove away.

Mac had by far the toughest time. He had chosen the longest swim and wished he hadn't. It was right round Greenwich Reach and into Blackwall Reach, and an exit in Bow Creek. Each leg movement pumped blood from both wounds, and he felt cold and sick by the time he struggled out of his kit and dumped it under the bridge at Lower Lea Crossing. He climbed out only with great effort, crossed the railway line, and stumbled to his car in Victoria Dock Road. He had to rest for half an hour and could feel himself falling asleep, so he drove unsteadily off through Canning Town and out through East London to join the A12 route to East Anglia. The seventy five mile drive back to Suffolk was a nightmare, nearly falling asleep at the wheel several times. It was dawn before he collapsed into bed, his wife frantic at his wounds, blood-soaked clothes, and white, haggard appearance.

Rod had planned the shortest swim for himself. He had to get back to the party on board the Galatea as soon as possible. He let the Prospect of Whitby pub go by then swam to the mouth of the Shadwell Basin. He dumped his kit, climbed out underneath Wapping Wall Bridge, and quickly pulled on a shirt, jeans and trainers from a small dry-bag and threw it away. Walking fast along Wapping High Street he passed the Police Headquarters still ablaze with lights, cars outside and boats revving at the pontoon. If anyone saw him they paid no attention.

He jumped up onto the deck of the Theseus, into the cabin, took a lipstick and smeared some on his face, unzipped his jeans and picked up a case of champagne.

Back on the Galatea he called out loudly, "Hey! Some bloody party this is; it's all gone quiet. Come on, let's get into this lot!", and with a drunken laugh he fired a cork across the cabin breaking one of the lights. He swayed against the blonde beside him as his arm went round her waist. Later that night she had good cause to remember him. Rarely had she been made love to with such hard thrusting power. That she was someone else's wife didn't seem to concern her. They both fell into an exhausted sleep, but not before Rod had memorized her name. She certainly wouldn't forget his. She hadn't been laid so well for a long time.

Driving back from Windsor Castle, Chief Superintendent Playford had a very bad feeling about the hoax pulled on him. He didn't go home. Something told him to go to his Headquarters. Driving fast and expertly he cut through West London and took the Embankment route along the river. As early as Lower Thames Street he could see the glow of the Tower on fire and felt sick in his stomach. Byward Street and Tower Hill were jammed with emergency vehicles, and he had to take a long loop round Cable Street to reach his base. There he learned the worst. Or what they thought was the worst. The worst was yet to come.

Major General Meadows was very angry. He had never been treated so shabbily. It took him an hour to regain the Tower, and minutes of angry blustering before he could convince the cordon of deeply suspicious policemen that this purple-faced old man in the bright scarlet fancy dress was indeed the person charged with the protection of the Tower and it's contents. The scene of devastation which met his eyes left him aghast. His first thoughts were for the safety of the Crown Jewels, but it took an hour to control the fires, and a further hour to cool the twisted, red-hot steel structure that had once been the vaults.

The Police Commissioner was on the scene when it was possible to make a proper search of the debris and a final count. Several items of the regalia had been damaged by fire, some lighter pieces had melted, and the robes were gone completely. But there was no doubt about it, all the main crowns and scepters were missing.

The General drew himself up, "It is my sad duty to inform Her Majesty at once."

"No, Sir", replied the Commissioner, "I'm afraid you can't do that. As head of the government the Prime Minister must be informed first, and it is for him to inform Her Majesty."

"Damn you, Sir!", swore the General, "I know my duty. I am Her Majesty's personal representative in this her own fortress!"

"Very well, General, if you insist. I will provide you with a car and escort." The Commissioner turned to two Inspectors, "See to a car and escort for the General", and they led him away.

Once out of earshot, the Commissioner spoke into his police network radio, "The Commissioner here. The car carrying General Meadows is to take him to Scotland Yard and detain him in my suite there. See he makes no calls. He'll complain like hell but it won't be for long."

To a Deputy Commissioner he said, "Take over here, Jamieson. I can't call the P.M. on this one, I'll have to see him personally." He strode off across Tower Green through firemen coiling their hoses.

It was 3 a.m. when the Commissioner's car was allowed through the wrought iron gates of Downing Street and up to the door of No.10. The duty guard knew it must be something really big to bring the Old Man himself here at this hour.

The P.M. was not stupid. Having told the Commissioner not to disturb him till morning, it was pointless being irate with the man, it must be something important. Bleary-eyed and with a robe over his pajamas, the P.M. ordered tea and they sat in a small study.

The Commissioner looked grim, "This couldn't be told you over the phone, Prime Minister, and it can't wait till morning. The London Airport attack was a diversion. The Tower of London has been severely damaged by gunfire from HMS Belfast, and from the Crown Jewels the crowns and scepters are missing."

Sheer disbelief silenced the P.M. for several seconds, until he could only say quietly, "My God! How appalling. You're sure, Commissioner?"

"I'm afraid so, Sir. We have no leads yet except that it has some of the hallmarks of the I.R.A, and the river seems to have been the main means of escape." He added awkwardly, "Sir, the Governor of the Tower, General Meadows, insists on informing Her Majesty personally, but I have detained him briefly on my own authority."

"Thank you, Commissioner, that was wise. Yes, it is something I must do, and before the media reports reach her." He looked appalled, "My God, a task no Prime Minister has ever had to do. Can you imagine her reaction?"

"No, Sir, it's not a job I would relish."

"Right, Commissioner, thank you. I must get moving. Please give my Private Secretary updates hourly. I need hardly stress that all our jobs are on the line here."

He swept out of the room sending flying with a loud crash a tray of tea things being brought in.

On the phone to his Private Secretary the P.M. was shouting, "Yes, now! I know the time! Get on to Windsor and find out what is the earliest possible time Her Majesty will see me. Say it's a matter of the utmost national importance. No, it's not war, it's worse than that! Get a move on and call me back at once."

At 7.30 a.m. the Prime Minister's car plus escort sped into the grounds of Windsor Castle. The Queen had an intense dislike of pre-breakfast appointments. The jowled Hanoverian face was stern and unsmiling in it's non-public guise. She sat at a small gilded desk, and the P.M. made to take a chair.

"I did not invite you to sit, Prime Minister", she said in a cool, commanding voice.

He found himself shuffling like a schoolboy, "I regret to have to inform you, Ma'am, of an attack on the Tower of London and the removal of the main Crown Jewels."

The Queen's hand tightened on the desk, and the face hardened into a mask, "Give me the details as far as you know them."

"All the crowns except for Queen Victoria's miniature one are gone, they must have missed that; and all the scepters. Much of the rest is damaged by fire, Ma'am."

The Queen looked away and out over the park behind her. Then turned and fixed her eyes on him. He had never seen a more icily chilling stare from anyone, "Coming at this time, so close on events of recent and unwelcome memory with the death of Diana, this is a blow from which the monarchy might not recover. I need hardly tell you, Prime Minister, that I hold you responsible personally for the recovery of our Crown Jewels."

"Yes, Ma'am", he mumbled.

"Was anyone hurt?", she snapped.

"Not seriously, Ma'am."

"Thank God for that", and without any words of parting, she rose and made for a door which opened of it's own accord and disappeared through it.

In Hounslow, West London, Philip Turner had done exactly what he was told. He threw the mobile phone into a pond and went home to bed.

He got the thin, reedy greeting, "Is that you, Philip, dear?"

"Yes, mother", then under his breath "Who the hell would it be?"

But he couldn't sleep, and spilled his cocoa as his hands shook so much. He feared the worst. He always did.

CHAPTER 7: PURSUIT.

The news of the theft of the Crown Jewels could not be withheld. To say the media made a meal of it would be the understatement of all time. They went straight for the throat of those supposed to prevent such 'outrages'. The Prime Minister was pressed in Parliament like never before. Yes, the case would be prosecuted to the utmost, the offenders found and brought to justice. Promises were made because they had to be made. Results were demanded, and fast.

The police forensics people had found the small metal disc marked 'Remember 1916', which showed the marks of having been worn like an army dog-tag. In 1916 the British had very foolishly shot the Irishman Patrick Henry Pearse and his comrades for their part in the Dublin Easter Rising. This made them heroes and martyrs in the eyes of all Irish Republicans, and a rallying cry ever since for Irish anti-British feeling. The same words could still be seen sprayed on walls in Northern Ireland. The Muslim Brotherhood notes had clearly been decoys to concentrate security forces around the airport in West London and away from the Tower. The I.R.A's plan had worked well. Reaction times to the events at the Tower had been slow and very inadequate.

The Commissioner called the most wide-ranging conference ever seen in Britain's police forces. All provincial Chief Constables were called to London. All Department Heads in the Metropolitan Police were told to drop what they were doing and attend. All leave was canceled. The hunt went nationwide at once. Interpol were brought in. Clearly gemstones of the size taken could not be cut without world-class expert help. The Amsterdam underworld at once fell under close scrutiny.

In essence, all county and city police forces were told to drop everything they possibly could. All other inquiries must become secondary to recovering the Crown Jewels. All leads must be followed up, no matter how flimsy. The best ideas men must be put on the job, not just the routine plodders. Some bright people had beaten the nation's best defenses; it would take bright people to think the same way. Reject no proposal, no matter how far-fetched. Somewhere there will be a lead.

"I need hardly tell you, gentlemen", said the Commissioner, "That if we don't crack this one, and quickly, we'll be a laughing stock for years to come."

In turn each senior officer present briefed their subordinates, and so on down to street level. It became by far the biggest man-hunt in British criminal history.

The wrecked escape boat with it's burnt-out outboards led to the white BMW, and the old folks' 'eye-witness' accounts, all useless, of four young men making good their escape. The woman traffic warden glowed with pride at having put the police onto the real criminals, led by a very rude man of whom she could give no clear description; and would she get the huge reward offered by the tabloid press?

Within hours the Calais police reported the car. Yes, it had been towed away from the station forecourt and was in their police compound now. Yes, they would hold it while a transporter came to collect it, but typical of French bureaucracy, the release fee would have to be paid to keep their books straight.

Now it was a Europe-wide search, and becoming a world-wide one. Clearly these criminals had major financial backing. The Mafia perhaps? A fanatical and immensely rich jewel collector?

Days passed and the clamor for revelations grew ever more intense. The government must be seen to be doing something, anything. In Parliament the mood was ugly.

Heads must roll. Quite undeservedly General Meadows found himself retired early, with thanks for his years of devoted service, and a routine minor decoration. The man who replaced him was a distinguished combat veteran. Chief Superintendent Playford was transferred to F5 Division, Personnel and Training, so his 'years of experience could be of benefit to incoming recruits'. He was a broken man and he knew it. He took a long sick leave then voluntary early retirement. The Commissioner made sure the pension didn't suffer.

Some did better. The Tower's Guard Commander was promoted and decorated for his dash and courage. 'Sword Against Guns!' raved the tabloid press. But his bent, shattered arm, and lopsided, wired-up jaw made him unfit for active service. He languished thereafter on office work. His word as an officer and a gentleman was not doubted, but where was the sword he claimed to have used? And if he had used it as he described, inflicting a mortal thrust through the body of an attacker, surely there would be copious bloodstains where the man fell?

The police did not let the public in on the real answer. By taking away the blood-covered blade, and by applying a very intense fire to the site of the incident, no blood samples could be taken by their forensic people; thus no DNA matching could tie anyone into the raid.

The Chief Yeoman Warder, a colorful man much admired by the tourists for his military swagger and magnificent mustaches, and who would have given his life had he known how to do it, was retired and replaced. The new Chief Yeoman Warder was the Warrant Officer known universally in the Army as the worst bastard for discipline and absolute devotion to the letter of Queen's Regulations.

None of this placated the public's anger at apparent police incompetence, and search warrants flew like confetti. Every boat in St. Katherine's Dock was searched like never before. The movements of everyone had to be accounted for at midnight on 26th July. Half the harbor had been partying on the Galatea, and all could confirm each other's stories. The married woman was convinced she had spent most of the night being made love to by her magnificent stallion of a man. Rod's alibi was unshakable.

He went home and shaved off his mustache.

"Oh, that's much better, darling", said Susan. "Wasn't that a dreadful business about the Crown Jewels? Could you see anything from the boat?"

Superintendent John Cooper thought the escape boat and white BMW were all too convenient. The attackers had used a decoy to get in, they would use a decoy to get out. The BMW was a 'plant'.

The attackers had to be ex-service personnel, quite likely Marines; they had all the right skills. And not young ones either. These people knew about out-dated naval warships and their gunnery, so the men, or some of them, came from that era.

The conference called by Cooper's Divisional Commander had an air of desperation about it. No one on the force had been able to come up with leads of any kind. They were grasping at straws. When the audience was asked for contributions, there was a long and embarrassing silence. It seemed to go on for minutes, with people looking round at each other hoping someone would say something.

Cooper's voice broke the silence quietly but in such a way that it couldn't have been more effective.

He said simply, "It all begins in Bombay."

You could hear a pin drop. People turned to stare in surprise. They knew about his odd-ball reputation, but they weren't scornful, his record was too good. They just didn't understand.

"Explain, please", said the Commander.

Cooper produced the report from India of some months ago and read the key points. He went on, "These people can't steal the ammo they need in Britain, it hasn't been made here for years. Army stuff won't fit, that's 155 mm in caliber and not armor-piercing. So they've got to steal the ammo from somewhere that's got it. Where do old British warships go to die? The Commonwealth. The last users of this ammo were India. I've checked. It has a storage life of at least twenty years. The theft in India was reported as connected to Kashmir. I say the shells used in HMS Belfast probably came from Bombay, and it ought to be checked out."

There was another long silence while they took it all in. No one else in the room would have made the mind-leap to connect a domestic robbery to events across the other side of the world. But the Commissioner had given orders to follow up all leads, however tenuous.

The Commander said "Thank you, Superintendent. Get out there at once, and I mean leave today. Take an assistant if you need one."

Half the room swiveled round towards Cooper hoping to be chosen for a freebie to India.

But Cooper replied, "Thank you, Sir, I'll leave at once, but I'll do better on my own."

He would too. He knew no one in the Division who had the same quirky thought processes, or the ability to concentrate with quite such microscopic intensity on one tiny piece of information. He rose and left. He didn't even go home. His passport was in his desk. Within an hour he was on his way to the airport, and an hour later on a flight to Bombay.

A week after the raid Rod took the Theseus out of St. Katherine's Dock and downriver. Boat movements in and out of the dock had continued unabated. After all, it was August and the busy summer season, so his departure aroused no interest. She could be operated single-handed if care was taken, and nothing unusual expected in the way of boat handling. Surging along in the Thames Estuary at a steady eight knots the whole world felt good.

He took the boat up the east coast and in past Felixstowe Docks to moor up for the night off Shotley

Marina. The next day he moved up the coast to Lowestoft, and alongside the Johnson's yard where she had been made ready for sea some months before.

Rod found Bert Johnson and said, "Can you haul her out for me and scrape her clean? She's got a bit of growth; costing me a knot or two."

"Sure, we can do that for you, glad to."

Rod added, "And I'd like to change her name; I don't like Theseus any more."

Bert frowned, "Ah, well, you know that's bad luck, don't you, Sir?"

"Yes, but I'll risk it", said Rod. "I'd prefer a girl's name. What do you suggest? My wife's called Agnes so I don't fancy that. How about your wife's name?"

"That's kind of you, Sir", replied Bert, "But my wife's Dutch and you wouldn't believe her handle. My little girl's got a nice name though, Crystal, how would that do?"

"Yes, perfect", said Rod, "Let's call her that. Put it across her stern and both bows."

Bert smiled, "My little girl will be pleased when I tell her we've got a boat at the yard being named after her. When do you want the boat, Sir?"

"I need her soon please", said Rod, "I want to get some more fishing charters out on her while the weather's still good."

"Two or three days, say three days is the best I can do."

"OK I'll come for her in three days, see you then", said Rod and walked off down the quayside.

The Queen had asked for daily reports on progress from the Prime Minister to be delivered personally, but these had lapsed to weekly as it became clear there was no news. She was deeply displeased at her government's inability to recover the Crown Jewels. They were, after all, her personal possessions, not those of the State. She conveyed her displeasure in a subtle but powerful way. She withheld her assent from an honors list of political

100

party lackeys and senior government time-servers submitted to her for the usual formality of her signature. No monarch had left such a list unsigned for over a century. The message, though unspoken, was entirely clear; no more civil honors until her Crown Jewels were recovered.

The Commissioner's Divisional Heads had all the leads being followed up, but the trail was cold. The I.R.A had clearly used their biggest mortars on the airport while the Belfast was shelling the Tower. It was known that the I.R.A made their big mortars by cutting the tops off gas cylinders, and their shells were big fire extinguisher bodies filled with home-made high explosives. This time they must have used Semtex to get the effect they did.

What was puzzling though was the cool nerve of the crew who had fired the mortars from the back of a truck. Normally the I.R.A used a timer and were long gone when their mortars fired. This time though they had aimed with care, fallen short, and adjusted their aim twice. Their attempts to hit the Terminal buildings or parked aircraft had mercifully failed. Heaven knows what might have happened if their mortars had enough range. It was typical bungling by I.R.A amateurs, they hadn't used enough propellant. They must have been nervous about blowing up their crude gas cylinder barrels. It was just their good luck that they had hit a runway and some fuel tankers. But to get clear away with their truck was unusually clever of them. It was probably hidden in a garage or barn somewhere and might never be found, if it hadn't been burned already. Intensive searches for it were in constant progress, working out from the airport perimeter. They had got fifteen miles so far. They were confident they'd find it in the end. It was just a matter of time.

Mac's thigh healed steadily. He refused flatly to have any medical treatment and tended his own wounds. It was a sheer fluke that the sword blade had scraped the upper femur bone and passed between it and the femoral artery. Had that been severed Mac would have been a goner. He was walking on the beach now, limping slightly. His regular customers were glad to see him about again after so stupidly putting a garden fork through his foot.

Professor Julian Carbery, FRS, was Master of University College, Oxford. As Master of President Clinton's Oxford College, Carbery had enjoyed the media attention during the President's visit with Hillary back to his old College. But Carbery was better known in academic circles as Britain's most distinguished marine biologist. Living in the inland city of Oxford he habitually took his vacations along parts of Britain's coastline or those abroad. Thus he was in Lowestoft walking along the quayside looking at the fishing nets. They were often a good source of interesting finds, specially the beam trawls which worked along the sea bed.

He stopped suddenly and went completely rigid, "My God! I don't believe it!" He fumbled in a pocket and drew spectacles from a battered case. He peered closely through thick lenses at the stern of a boat, below the waterline and near an outlet pipe.

He gasped, "It is! It's Stigeoclonium Mumbaii. Amazing!"

He took out a small pocket knife, scraped at the hull and folded something carefully into a handkerchief. He then scribbled some lines in a small note book. There was an old bearded boatyard worker scraping the next boat along.

Carbery called out to him, "I say, my man! Where is this boat from?" He pointed to the Theseus.

The old man replied, "She's an east coast boat, Sir, as far as I know; she's worked from here as long as I've been here, and that's fifteen years."

Carbery asked, "Are the waters here unusually warm?"

The old man relished this stranger's ignorance, "Well, Sir, it's Sizewell Nuclear Power Station, you see; first one reactor, then a second, and there's even talk of a third. But I don't like 'em, ain't natural. Look what they've done to the sea round here. There's millions of gallons a day of hot water goes into the sea and it's warmed it all up for miles around. You should see some of the fish they catch now, big puffer fish and all sorts of sharks; I've seen 'em myself."

"Yes, yes, thank you, thank you", said Carbery and walked away.

Clearly this maritime yokel was going to go on at length and Carbery had heard enough. He was the one used to being listened to. There would certainly be an article in his important find; a learned paper to enhance his reputation. It might even grace the pages of 'Nature', Britain's most respected ecological journal. What a coup for him.

An hour later the scrapers got to work on the Theseus and her name disappeared.

Superintendent Cooper needed less than forty eight hours in Bombay. At the Indian Police Headquarters, Chief Inspector Naupada was certainly interested in Cooper's reasons for being there and was as helpful as possible, but there wasn't much to go on. In essence, as Naupada outlined it, the raid on the Naval Depot clearly needed organization, skill and timing. It wasn't a job done by opportunists. Only two crime outfits in Bombay could provide that kind of back-up; the Duleep family who ran most of the drugs business, prostitution and protection rackets in the area, and taking explosives wasn't really in their line of work. Then there was Kapoor and his lot. They could have done it as we've got a bank job and a mail van robbery down to them, but the police have never got anything on Kapoor. He was too clever, always two or three removes from any action. If underlings were taken they never talked. If they did, they got their throats cut, even in prison.

Yes, some ex-naval person probably helped them find the stuff, but who? There were hundreds in the Bombay area alone, and where would you start? No, we don't have everyone on computer like you do. There were a billion people in India by the last census. There were twelve and half million in Greater Bombay alone. We have the biggest slum in Asia here, the Dharavi, with conditions you wouldn't believe. We did find a burnt-out ex-army truck on a beach not far from the Depot after the raid, and one like it was used by the thieves, but it could have been a decoy. The ammunition could have left by sea, but I think it more likely went inland into the hills; they're full of caves. Yes, we did check engine and chassis numbers on the truck, and it was released to a surplus dump a year ago. No, they didn't have a record of who bought it. It was probably a cash sale, and they wouldn't tell us anyway as the tax people have been chasing them.

Yes, I can get you a record of all vessels which stayed in Bombay for the period of the raid, but I must point out that if anyone was going to lift ammunition from a beach, they could approach the coast from out at sea and leave the same way without ever putting into port here. That would be the sensible way, wouldn't it?

Cooper listened attentively to all the Chief Inspector's reasoning, and couldn't argue with any of it. It was all entirely plausible.

Cooper said, "Could you let me have a car and driver for a day? Someone who can show me the harbor, the Naval Depot and the beach? I'd like to get the feel of the places you mentioned."

"Certainly, I'll organize that for you now", said the Chief Inspector. He called in a smartly dressed Constable who led Cooper outside.

It was August and the monsoon was in full flow. Bombay got 63 inches of rain through July and August, more than the wettest parts of Britain got in a year. Added to this was the 90 degree heat and Cooper felt he was in a steam bath. The Indians were used to it, but in his unsuitable English clothing Cooper ran sweat from every pore.

The harbor gave a flavor not just of rank odors, but of myriad small workshops in ramshackle sheds where any work could be done and no records kept. The Naval Depot had only barbed wire and toy soldiers guarding it. He could see none of the cameras and detection devices which would surround any arsenal in the western world. The beach site still contained the wreck of the burnt-out truck, now red with rust. No tracks remained, beaten down by the relentless rain. Out to sea the Arabian Ocean went on for ever. He could see the curvature of the earth.

Back at Bombay Police Headquarters, Cooper thanked the Chief Inspector for his help, collected the typed list of vessels, and left for the airport.

In Lowestoft, Rod collected the Crystal, paid his bill in cash, and set out to sea. This time he turned North along the Norfolk coast and put in for the night at King's Lynn. The next day he took her up to Hull. At the yard of Humber Breakers Ltd, Rod sold her for a deal less than he gave. The government was paying grants to take fishing boats out of commission on condition they were cut up as proof. Breakers were buying up boats for the amount of the grant, and made their profit on selling the engines and other gear out of the boats. Rod asked how long it would take.

"Oh, she'll be gone in a day or two. We don't hang about. No use having your money tied up in rusting steel, is there?"

Rod looked close to tears as he walked away. The breaker's man was used to seeing fishing skippers like that, men who couldn't take the wrench from their life's work. He didn't see Rod's smile as he got out of sight.

And so the Theseus, now the Crystal, disappeared for ever.

A week later some photos were collected from the camera shop in Pakefield Road, Lowestoft. In them was a grinning little girl perched on her father's shoulder. She was pointing up proudly to her own name painted on the stern of a steel motor fishing vessel.

Cooper's flight home was tiresome but the air-conditioning was blissfully cool. There was time to study the list of shipping. It was long and complex: name, flag flown, registered tonnage, cargo or private, date in, date out, cargo carried, and so on. Cooper ticked those shown as British and studied their details; commercial cargo vessel or private venture? They would all need to be checked.

Reporting in London next day he outlined what he had, and admitted it was a long shot, but he'd like to check it out. He had some other ideas as well, and got the approval he needed. Anything would get approval. Why should his ideas be worse than any others, and at least his record was good. The police were even listening to mediums and psychics now.

Cooper put a team onto tracing the movements of all the British vessels on the Bombay list, and their present whereabouts. The records of all Royal Marines were pulled who were retired and between 30 and 60 years old. From these the Special Boat Service people were to be short-listed, and from those the Officers. All the S.B.S were skilled and resourceful, but planning and leadership of a high order had been shown, so they would start with the Officers and work back from there. The same was done for the S.A.S. They refused to comply at first, and it took a call from the Prime Minister to the Army Chief of Staff to get it done. He phoned the S.A.S Headquarters at Hereford and ordered them to co-operate.

The film from the security cameras at London Airport had been studied a hundred times. Nothing. Every discernible face for the relevant time-span had been checked against central records at Scotland Yard, and no identifiable person could be seen. Cooper asked to see the films and pored over them for hours. Again and again he ran them back. Gradually a feeling grew that there was something not quite right. It kept nagging at him but he couldn't solve it. Then suddenly it was there. The missing piece fell into place.

He called over the other people in the room, and ran the film for them. They stared blankly at the screen as the figures moved about. The moment when the first tremors shook the airport buildings, then the second, then the third and the fireball's flash becoming visible and people scurrying for the exits.

Cooper asked, "Well? What do you see? What's odd in those pictures?"

A blank silence from the audience. No one had anything to say.

Cooper said gently, "What month was it?"

The audience exchanged glances of disbelief. One said, "July."

"Well?", persisted Cooper, "Is that midsummer or midwinter?"

Someone humored him with, "Midsummer."

"Well then", said Cooper pointing with a pencil, "Why is this man wearing gloves?"

There was an audible gasp from the group.

One exclaimed, "So he is! Now there's a guy who doesn't want to leave any prints."

Cooper responded, "Exactly. Now watch his movements. There are plenty of people using mobile phones in any airport as in our film here, but this man isn't ringing his wife or girlfriend. He uses his phone three times, and each time so briefly he can't have said more than five words. And he's looking out over the airport."

Cooper paused for effect, "Now, look at the timing of those calls. He answers it once. He's nervous. He nearly drops the bag. There's the first explosion. He doesn't move, he stays put, it's as though he's expecting it. He calls a number and speaks briefly. Thirty seconds later there's the second explosion. And still he doesn't move, although people all around him are beginning to panic. He calls again, speaks a few words, then turns to go and moves off this camera. Thirty seconds later the third explosion happens."

There was a long, slow pause of realization from the group round him.

Cooper said quietly, "This is no I.R.A job from nearby. This man is a spotter for the Tower attack. Half a minute is the flight time for a shell from the Belfast to the airport."

Someone behind Cooper said, "Bloody hell!"

Cooper spoke purposefully, "We need this man and we need him fast. I want full computer enhancement of his face, lip readers to give us what he says, and a readout of the numbers he hit on his phone. Get moving!"

It was the first spark of light. His Commander phoned the Commissioner who phoned the P.M. "Prime Minister, we have our first real lead. The film from the airport has given us a possible suspect. We're working on it now."

"Thank God for that, Commissioner. At last. Give me something, anything. Her Majesty is now withholding her co-operation in legislation, which constitutionally she can do. Government is becoming increasingly difficult. You must crack this case soon!"

The word on the street amongst those who knew, the minor criminal fraternity, was that it was pointless looking. Over his beer, one summed it up, "Nah, you ain't gonna find nuffink. It was a done deal right from the start. You can't fence rocks like that. Some rich guy paid for the job and he's got 'em at home now, gloating over 'em."

All the police's criminal contacts were tried, and pressure applied, including the Mafia. Rocco Traficante was of the opinion that no gem cutter in Europe could split up the Crown Jewels without them hearing about it, and he had heard nothing. And he would have heard.

In Parliament, two widely differing schools of thought began to develop. One said the crime was so monstrous it warranted suspension of the law of Habeus Corpus. Such a course was taken only in wartime, and would give the government powers of search and arrest without trial. The opposing view had begun to say what was all the fuss about? So what if some crowns and scepters had been stolen? They weren't really important in themselves. The resources being devoted to their recovery were out of all proportion to their value. Meanwhile the crime rate soared as criminals went on the spree, fairly safe in the knowledge that they wouldn't be caught.

Public opinion too was becoming divided. There were suggestions in the right-wing media that if the Crown Jewels were not recovered, then it was the nation's loyal duty to make amends for it's incompetence by replacing the regalia as far as possible. This outraged the left-wing media. It was disgraceful that the poor working classes might be taxed to replace such pointless baubles. The monarchy was rich enough. The Queen was the world's wealthiest woman. Let them buy their own trinkets.

This polarity in society grew steadily stronger. The Crown Jewels had become a cause. The perpetrators could be seen perhaps as heroes. Clearly they were not mere thieves. They had been very selective. The crowns and scepters were the key symbols of royal power. They had left behind much of great value that mere criminals would have taken. They had done some damage to the Tower of London, but that a symbol of royal oppression through the ages, a place of cruelty and torture. They had caused no deaths and clearly had sought to avoid doing so. If greed was not their motive then, what was it? Was there a higher reason? Perhaps it was to cause the monarchy to be brought into question and re-examined as system fit for a supposedly self-governing nation.

Cooper cleared his desk as the shipping list analysis arrived. Red stars had been put against two vessels. The Dauntless carrying sisal matting, ropes and fenders had put into Tilbury in the Thames well before the Tower job, and left again within forty eight hours to return to Bombay with a cargo of tractor spares.

The second vessel jumped out from the page: Theseus, St. Katherine's Dock, and there over the period of the raid! Present whereabouts unknown.

Cooper ordered, "Find that boat! I don't care what it takes. But don't blunder about. I want to creep up on these people. They're not fools. Make your inquiries as discreet as you can. Always plain clothes, no uniforms. Get going."

The Royal Marines and Special Air Service lists had arrived. The choice of Officers in both cases was. surprisingly small. They really were elites. Cooper gave instructions to go to the homes of the Officers first, and trace their movements on the night in question. And to do it without giving offense.

The police forensics laboratories had given the airport films the full treatment, but were not hopeful about the results. The suspect had worn a cap, and with head lowered or partly turned away it had not been possible to get an accurate lip-read from the film. And the gloves obscured the times he had dialed the phone. Some numbers were discernible but not enough to be a traceable sequence.

The face had been enhanced enough to result in a vague police artist's impression, and this was circulated at once nationwide. Philip Turner nearly died of fright when he saw it. Panic stricken, he took to sunglasses at once, and began to grow a weedy mustache. His mother said it made him look more like executive material. He called in sick and took the two weeks of vacation owing to him. He spent it at home working in the garden. He only went out at night, and then just to the corner shop.

Suddenly two things came together. The St. Katherine's Dock register gave the home port of the Theseus as Lowestoft in Suffolk. Only one retired Royal Marine S.B.S Officer aged between 30 and 60 lived along that coast. They had a name.

Cooper led the visiting police team himself. He had a search warrant. He had phoned ahead to check that Captain Jackson was in. The house was being watched from a distance so there was no risk of flight. Jackson was friendly and helpful. Yes, he had owned a boat called the Theseus but had sold it to a man called Larsen in King's Lynn. He had received cash for it and his bank would confirm a deposit of that amount recently. No, Rod didn't know anything about Larsen, except that he had a slight Scandinavian accent. Rod said he felt lucky to sell as fishing boats were falling in value as quotas got less, but other European nations seemed able to make their fishing pay, and were buying up cheap boats in Britain.

Rod was asked to detail his movements with the Theseus over the summer, specially the period of 26th July. He explained the extended cruise along the English Channel to Cornish waters for fishing and scuba diving, then the cruise back along the French coast. Alone? No, with an ex-Marine friend, Mac Maclean who ran the pub at Felixstowe Ferry.

Cooper asked politely, "Would you mind if we looked around please?"

Rod paused, so Cooper added, "We do have a search warrant."

So Rod had to agree. The search was perfunctory on purpose, taking only a few minutes.

Cooper asked, "Where is your wife, Sir?"

"She plays golf three days a week at various courses round here, probably at Woodbridge today."

Cooper concluded cheerfully, "Well, thank you for help, Sir. Oh, one last thing. Would you mind coming with us to Felixstowe Ferry to show us where Mr. Maclean lives, and it will save time as I'm sure he can confirm your account."

"Sure, not at all", said Rod pleasantly. He joined Cooper in the car and they drove off.

As the car turned the corner a dark blue van pulled out of the Maybush Inn car park and stopped at Rod's house. Eight men in overalls jumped out. Four virtually took Rod's Land Rover to pieces. Four went into the house. Two set about bugging the phones, and each room without a phone, and two men made an expert search. They drilled tiny holes in floorboards and walls and inserted viewing devices, tapped the backs of all cupboards, looked under all drawers, felt down into the water tank in the attic, looked into each toilet cistern, checked under baths and around fireplaces for traps. It was quick, thorough and professional. No visible traces remained. Finger prints were taken at several places.

Mac played it beautifully. They hadn't got a warrant for his place, but they were welcome to look. And by the way, if they saw any rats would they knock 'em on the head as there were several that lived in the cellar. Mac's account of the summer cruise was just the right amount off perfect not to sound glib.

Apparently satisfied, Cooper returned Rod to his house, thanked him for his help and left.

Round the corner, Inspector Fredericks joined Cooper in his car.

Fredericks said, "Nothing in the house, Sir, but the car was useful. These were in the tread of the spare tire."

Fredericks handed Cooper a small polythene sample bag. From it he tipped two tiny black objects into his palm.

Cooper exhaled with satisfaction, "Aaaah!", then rhetorically, "How many people do we know, Inspector, with typewriter letters in their tires? This man has been running over a typewriter. We don't see them lying about, do we? I'm beginning to get a feeling about our Captain Jackson. Much too self-assured for me. I'll lay odds these little beauties match the typeface on the decoy letters sent to the Governor of the Tower and the Chief Superintendent."

The convoy raced down the A12 highway to London.

The Theseus had disappeared completely. No trace of her in Britain or abroad could be found, nor of a Larsen answering to Rod's description. Had she been scuttled at sea? The team charged with finding her were not allowed to give up. They were told to keep looking till they came up with something, anything.

In normal times the Prime Minister's weekly visits to brief the Queen on routine political matters were fairly amicable; they sat in easy chairs and chatted over tea or coffee. These talks usually went into abeyance while the royal family was at Balmoral in Scotland for their summer holiday, and were replaced by phone conversations. Now though, the Queen insisted that the P.M. flew weekly to Scotland to brief her on progress with the investigations. He could hardly refuse to go, even though it took him a whole day each time. This meant he got no break of more than a few days during the whole summer recess of Parliament.

The Queen had remained very cool during all such meetings since the loss of her Crown Jewels, and he had come to dread them. Queen Victoria had disliked her Prime Minister, Gladstone, and refused to allow him to sit in her presence, even for meetings of over two hours and when he was an old man of over eighty. Now Elizabeth did the same to her Chief Minister.

She opened haughtily, "What news have you to tell me, Prime Minister?"

She made the title sound like an underling. He reported on what they had so far, which was precious little, trying to draw optimism from the few leads being followed, but no arrests were foreseen.

Then she spoke about what was really on her mind, "Have you considered, Prime Minister, what we are going to wear at the forthcoming State Opening of Parliament?"

Damn! He'd never thought of it in all the press of his work, "Er, no Ma'am, I'm afraid I haven't", he apologized lamely, "We could make a perfect replica of the Imperial State Crown, I'm sure, Ma'am."

She lifted an eyebrow and replied icily, "One does not wear replicas."

There was an awkward silence while he couldn't think of anything to say, and wished he wasn't there.

She went on, "I must tell you candidly, Prime Minister, that I do not relish in the least taking part in that occasion. Television will highlight no doubt the fact that I have none of the real crowns, and certainly not the Imperial State Crown one has always worn. All that survives in a wearable condition, I understand, is Queen Victoria's miniature crown. Are you aware that she wore it only as a widow after Prince Albert's death, and it was placed on her coffin when she died? It has never been used at a Coronation or State Opening of Parliament."

"Er, no Ma'am, I was not aware of that", he mumbled.

"We need hardly tell you, Prime Minister, that the monarch is not only royal but regal, and to be seen as anything less than that on a great State occasion seems to us to be personally demeaning. To put it bluntly, if we are to appear as your Sovereign then we should have the proper accoutrements of sovereignty. I'm sure you agree?"

Never had such a question demanded anything but, "Yes, Ma'am."

She went on, "Victoria's crown is tiny, only three and a half inches across, smaller than a saucer. It would look ridiculous on me, and I regard it as deeply distasteful that I might have to wear it at the State Opening. I'm sure you agree."

"Yes, Ma'am."

"Redouble your efforts, Prime Minister, and bring me good news on your next visit. Good day to you."

And he was dismissed, beads of sweat forming on his brow.

The flight back to London was not pleasant. She was right of course. The State Opening of Parliament was the one occasion in the whole year when the Queen appeared in full splendor, robed, crowned, and enthroned before both Houses of Parliament, with the people watching on national television. None of the regalia which made the State Opening such a grand and colorful event would be present. In particular the Imperial State Crown, the largest and most impressive of the crowns, with it's spectacular diamonds, would be specially conspicuous by it's absence.

There seemed to be no end to this damned problem. The Queen would confer no civil honors on anyone. She would invest only military decorations for heroism, and there weren't any. The pressure from the civil service and his party backers was becoming intolerable. Senior people were not getting the knighthoods and peerages they felt they had earned over time, or for which they had paid heavily. Right down through society, all the middle men, worthies and functionaries who looked for their public recognition as a matter of course were disappointed and angry. This ill feeling was directed naturally at the government and police for their continuing incompetence. But one thing the Prime Minister did know; he didn't want many more interviews like the one he'd just had.

At Scotland Yard, the two pieces of typeface were found to be an 'e' and a 'k'. Neither of the bogus letters sent to General Meadows or Chief Superintendent Playford had a 'k' in them, but there were plenty of 'e's. The 'e' found in Captain Jackson's tire made a good match with the 'e's in the letters. It was another step forward, but was it conclusive? The typeface was a common one. Many thousand such typewriters had been made and sold, and many were still in service. Was it possible to pick up such pieces of typeface accidentally in a tire? Cooper decided to check it out for himself.

On a map of Suffolk county, Cooper marked the nearest public waste disposal site to where Jackson lived in the village of Waldringfield. It was in Foxhall Road on the way to Ipswich, only five miles from Jackson's house. That's where people in the area disposed of unwanted household junk. It was a long shot of course. Jackson could easily have buried the typewriter or thrown it in the river. In an unmarked car, and casually dressed, Cooper drove into the site. It seemed quite well run. Each container was labeled clearly for it's purpose. The ones for metal scrap were on the left as he drove in. He parked and walked over to the big steel waste bins. Many small metal items lay around on the ground, screws, pieces of wire, washers, and so on. Anyone driving in might pick up something in their tires. He asked a site worker what happened to metal scrap.

"Get's baled up, mate. Goes in the crusher over there. Then goes off by truck to get melted somewhere. Birmingham way, I think."

Cooper asked, "Do you get many typewriters thrown away here?"

"Oh yeah, a dozen a week, minimum. Useless they are, we can't sell 'em on." The man spat on the ground, "Nah, we do OK from some of the furniture left here, but typewriters ain't no good to us, we just junk 'em."

So there it was. Jackson had probably broken up the typewriter in his garage, dropped some pieces on the floor and not noticed it. There was no typewriter and no proof that he had owned one with the type matching the bogus letters, nor that he had typed and sent them. It was just another piece in the puzzle gradually coming together.

But where was that bloody boat? The police search team had hit Lowestoft again as they moved round all the ports, concentrating in particular on the east coast ones. They must have interviewed about a third of the town's population. Yes, several people recalled the Theseus. No, they didn't know her whereabouts. Yes, they'd get in touch if they heard anything.

It had been a bad year for the Johnson's boat yard. There was very little business; they were barely covering their costs. So while the weather was still reasonable, the yard had shut for a long break. With luck there might be some oil rig repair work on their return. So there was no one at the yard for the police to interview. They moved along the quay to the next business and continued their inquiries.

Rod knew he was under surveillance. The police teams were quite good but he could spot some of the signs. Taking a drink in his local pub, the Maybush, he noticed strangers taking a more than casual interest in him. He knew his phones and house would be bugged, but that was no problem, he never talked by phone to anyone on his team. He went sailing in his boat, a 30 footer, which he had named 'Perhaps' after the Royal Marine joke about their motto, Per Mare, Per Terram, Perhaps. His usual trip in the boat was out to sea round the Cork Sand and back on the flood tide. Each time he did this he noticed a helicopter from the base at RAF Wattisham just visible in the distance, no doubt on a 'training exercise'.

He didn't search for the bugs in his house, to do so would give the game away. His Land Rover too he knew had received the full treatment. Several rattles and squeaks had disappeared where panels had been replaced and re-tightened up to the handbook torque. Parts of the vehicle were too clean where careful policemen had wiped away signs of their visit. Rod had told his wife about the police visit because if he hadn't done so she would have learned about it from people in the village, and that would create suspicion in her mind. It was just routine, he had said, he was at a party in St. Katherine's Dock on the night of the Tower incident, and they wanted to confirm someone else's story.

Rod never phoned Mac and didn't visit him for several weeks. When he did, he made sure it was on a day with a near gale of wind blowing. After a good lunch and some general chat, they went for a walk on the beach. Rod led them down the steep shingle slope to the water's edge. The heavy surf crashed ashore with a continuous roaring noise. It was hard to hear each other speak. It was certainly impossible for any directional listening devices to pick up what they said, no matter how sensitive. With their faces turned seawards they talked over reaction to the raid so far. Lip reading from a film taken through a long lens would see nothing.

Rod was calmly reassuring. It was all going to plan. The visit he got from the cops was entirely expected. They were just checking all ex-boots as a matter of routine because we're the best at that sort of job. They'd probably done the S.A.S as well. Yeah, the boat's gone for good, been cut up for scrap. So that's it, all we have to do now is be patient and wait for the right moment. It's all building up well. How's the leg? Mac's leg was fine. Got a twinge though when he gave Molly a good screwing. They both had a good laugh.

Professor Carbery was a happy man. His long vacation had led him to an important new discovery. Global warming was advancing at a much greater rate than previously estimated. As a distinguished marine biologist he was able to substantiate this claim with startling new evidence. His paper had been submitted to 'Nature', and to his delight accepted for publication on condition he shortened it by half. This he would do, though he felt he needed more space to argue his case fully. His reputation and the newsworthiness of his discovery had led to the acceptance of his work. But it would have to wait it's turn. It could not appear till the issue after Christmas. No matter, it would be an enormous coup for him when it came out. He allowed himself brief flirtations with the idea of becoming a Nobel Laureate. That was his greatest ambition. There would be no one else to share the enormous financial reward, nor dispute his sole claim to the discovery.

Carbery was one of that new breed of television scientists. He came from a theatrical family, and enjoyed appearing before the cameras. He felt he did it well. He had appeared twice already as a modern, presentable scientist. The paper in 'Nature' could only enhance his reputation and value in terms of the fees he could ask. He had told colleagues while dining at High Table in College of the forthcoming paper in 'Nature', but would not divulge it's contents.

"Congratulations, Master", said Dr. Mitchell with forced enthusiasm.

He was a historian who thought privately that anyone who made a career out of studying slime was a buffoon.

And Carbery was quite wrong, as he had been before. Stigeoclonium Mumbaii wasn't growing in the warming waters of the North Sea. The Theseus had picked up the growth in Bombay harbor, the only place it occurred. Hence the name, Mumbai was the Hindi for Bombay. The algae died in cold water, but Carbery had scraped the growth off her hull just aft of the hot water outlet from the engine. The boat had traveled back virtually non-stop to Britain. In the cooler Mediterranean the growth had begun to die and drop away. Through the yet colder Bay of Biscay and English Channel the process had accelerated. But in St. Katherine's Dock there was no tide. In the hot summer the air conditioners of the large office blocks all around emptied their water into the dock at near bath-water temperature. The Theseus had sat in a bath of luke-warm sea water for weeks. Thus the remaining algae around her engine outlet had survived. That found by Carbery after two days in the cold North Sea was the last vestiges of it before it too was about to fall away.

The State Opening of Parliament was a disaster. Not for the nation, but for the image of royalty. To the end the Queen refused to wear a replica of the Imperial State Crown. She insisted on wearing Queen Victoria's miniature crown, the only real one left. And Elizabeth was quite right. She did look ridiculous in it. It perched on top of her head like a small, shiny onion.

The Prime Minister's worst fears were realized. She was going to have her own say in the most public way. She changed the wording of the Queen's Speech, something never done by custom. It was always written by the government of the day, and merely read out by the reigning monarch from the throne. She had decided to add her own preamble. Of course no one could stop her. No one knew anything about it. Having made her entrance to the usual fanfare, she sat on the throne and took out her spectacles and put them on. Just at that moment the whole nation watching on television had the same impression. She looked just like a serious little old lady with a party hat on and about to read a shopping list. The grandeur was gone.

The stilted falsetto voice began, "We appear before you today as your Sovereign to do our customary duty of opening our Parliament. But we do so with some displeasure. We are displeased because the Crown Jewels are still absent. We charge my Lords and Commons with the loyal duty of recovering our regalia." The usual silence became tangibly, noticeably deeper.

Someone in the Press Gallery whispered audibly, "My God! She's gone too far this time."

The Queen then read the long list of legislation proposed for the forthcoming year in Parliament.

In the TV studios the commentators were stumbling for new adjectives. The Queen had openly criticized all of

Parliament and the government for their failures. She had implied this failure amounted to disloyalty to the Crown, and therefore to the nation. That was treason.

In it's replies the media did not pull any punches:

'Queen knocks the lot for failure to find sparklers!'
'Liz throws tantrum!'

In editorials, opinions hardened, 'Who does the Queen think she is? Millions in tax-payers' money is being spent on finding the jewels, and for what? For some colorful baubles for non-elected people to parade around in.'

Then came the inevitable comparisons. That amount of money would provide this amount of hospital beds, or that number of houses for the homeless, and so on. Opinion polls showed the country even more divided than before. About a third felt the Queen needed sympathy for being under great stress. The more vociferous and growing two thirds saw her as a petulant old woman who really thought it important that she had a proper crown to wear, thus telling millions of the poor that she understood nothing at all about the real conditions of life for the mass of her subjects.

That winter, just before Christmas, there had never been rain like it. For five days it rained more or less non-stop across southern England. The Thames Basin was just that, a basin. Into it drained an area of several hundred square miles. Water levels in the Thames Valley rose to danger level and serious flooding began to occur. All this water had only one place to go, down the River Thames. Nearly three months of rain had fallen in a few days. Millions of tons of water swelled the Thames to record levels. The Thames Barrier was designed to stop sea water coming up the river and flooding London. It could do nothing about floodwater coming down river, except to open it's sluices and hope that would be enough.

In the rain-lashed wheelhouse of his tug boat, Barney Cushman was cursing the weather. He grumbled a lot at the best of times, but now he was really sounding off. At over 70 and not very fit, he'd been lucky to keep his tug-master's ticket this year and he knew it. He'd be too weak soon to handle the heavy ropes, and his eyes were none too good either. He didn't relish the prospect of giving up on the river. He'd seen what happened to his old shipmates when they went ashore for good. They rotted away in some old folks' home. He'd taken on a new apprentice deck-hand this year. A willing lad he was, young Darren, but he knew nothing yet about how to work a barge. Still, he was cheap, and that was the main thing. He'd learn in time.

Barney's old tug, the Vulcan, had seen better days too. She was really on her last legs and wouldn't keep her certificate to operate much longer. The old Kelvin diesel needed a complete overhaul but he couldn't afford that. The only work he could get now was the odds and ends the bigger companies didn't want. So it was, in the driving rain, that he found himself contracted for the night movement of a full garbage scow from Chelsea Reach down river to the Power Station at Borthwick Wharf. With the 100 ton barge in tow, laden right to the gunwales, they made their way carefully downstream in the filthy black night. Darren's brew of coffee was good and strong, and they peered through the wheelhouse windows as the feeble wipers smeared the greasy glass.

Barney had not seen the river at this speed for years. A strong ebb tide with the full force of the floodwater behind it was pushing the barge along far quicker than he liked. With a crunch the barge nudged the stern of the Vulcan and she lurched and began to swing slightly. He opened the throttle and the tug shuddered under the unaccustomed revolutions. Black smoke belched from her stack.

Moving too quickly in the grip of the current, the barge just missed one of the uprights of Cannon Street rail bridge.

Barney cursed, "Bloody hell! That was close, too close for my liking."

But an oscillation had set up between the tug and the barge and they were swinging to and fro. The only way to kill the swing was for the tug to take control. Barney poured on the throttle and spun the wheel rapidly. There was no more skillful skipper on the river. With the speed rising inexorably the barge began to swing back again and Barney applied opposite helm.

"Come round, you bastard!", he swore.

From below came to the noise of grinding, tearing metal then silence. She'd seized! The massive granite piers of London Bridge, with their sharpened ends, loomed quickly into view.

Barney yelled, "Cast off, Darren, or we'll get crushed by the barge!"

Darren ran aft and began wrestling with the heavy wet ropes. The tug slewed as the inert propeller now acted like a water brake. Darren got two ropes off but the third was pulling tight as the barge and tug swung apart. Using all his strength he got one loop off the bollard before his foot slipped on the wet deck and he went down. The now singled-up rope ran off the bollard under the hundred-ton pull of the barge and the huge rope rasped Darren's hand off at the wrist like a grater through carrot. He shrieked and gripped the stump gouting arterial blood.

Barney abandoned the useless wheel and ran aft. He whipped off his scarf and tied it tightly round Darren's arm. There was a grinding crunch of steel on stone as the Vulcan hit one the piers of London Bridge and slid past. Luckily the barge had gone down the other side. The Vulcan, slewing helplessly, crashed heavily into the upstream end of the City Pier and was held there by the tide. Barney dragged Darren off the deck onto the pier and ran shouting for help towards London Bridge Hospital.

The barge, now spinning on it's axis, headed for Tower Bridge. How it missed the uprights was a miracle, but it was going to hit something. The Cherry Garden Pier by

Bermondsey Wall was half demolished by the hundred-ton blow it took, and the barge was kicked back out across the river.

In Wapping Police Station the Christmas Eve party was in full swing.

"Here's to crime!", called out a reveler as he raised his glass.

Then one of them yelled, "I don't believe it! Look at that!"

He pointed out across the river. The dark steel hulk of the barge was bearing down rapidly on the police pontoon.

"Get out!", shouted the new Superintendent.

But it was too late. As they ran downstairs they heard the grinding, squealing crash of steel on steel as the barge hit the upstream mooring pile and bent it over at forty five degrees. The barge veered round and scraped along the pontoon, brushing a patrol boat away from it as though it wasn't there. Stout mooring lines parted like string. The barge and unmanned patrol boat carried on downstream into the darkness.

The Superintendent acted quickly. Radio calls went out to the police boats patrolling downstream to retrieve the crew-less launch, and to alert shipping and shore installations about the rogue barge. It had to be stopped before the Thames Barrier or it could cause millions in damage.

A quick inspection of the police pontoon showed it might break away. It would have to be pulled further inshore and re-fastened. Sobering rapidly in the chilling rain, all hands heaved on the mooring lines and the pontoon eased closer in.

"She'll ground at low tide!", shouted one of the men.

The Superintendent replied, "A few days of that won't hurt it. She's built like a tank. Like a tank, get it?"

"Oh yeah, it's an oil tank", one man replied.

Out of earshot another muttered, "What a moron!"

The newly appointed Superintendent was young for his rank, and efficient. Thames Division needed a rising star after the debacle of the Tower incident. He would see to the repair of the mooring pile, and the lifting and checking of the pontoon in his usual quick and methodical way.

Meanwhile at each tide the heavy diesel-laden pontoon lowered itself ponderously onto the river bed, and onto the contents of the steel mesh sack beneath it. Cracks began to appear in the adhesive holding the steel anchor plates in place. They were not designed to take that kind of punishment.

The Queen's winter palace at Sandringham in Norfolk had not provided a happy Christmas for her. Her treatment by the media still rankled. She made her usual Christmas Day address to the nation and Commonwealth on television, but observers said her tone was less warm than of late. To the huge relief of the government she did not refer to the loss of the Crown Jewels, nor their inability to retrieve them. But unknown to her Ministers she had called a family conference. This decided that it's numerous members would do fewer public duties until the government was able to put right a situation seen as largely their own fault.

The New Year Honor's List was the smallest ever seen. Traditionally it was the time to reward the many hundreds of worthies throughout society. This time three servicemen were honored; a Sergeant for saving a colleague from drowning; a bomb disposal man for his bravery in Northern Ireland; and a helicopter pilot for a daring rescue. Two firemen were recognized for bravery, and some long-service awards made to Royal British Legion workers. And that was it. There were no peerages, no knighthoods, and none of the lesser civil orders. Only the Queen could confer these and she declined to do so. The message was clear.

The press picked skillfully on those deserving cases who missed out. Few minded that show business personalities or sportsmen went unrewarded, but the paymasters behind the political scenes were angry. It was their wives particularly who wanted to be Lady this or Countess that. The watchword of the party financiers became, 'No K, no pay', and contributions to party funds dried up. Charities lost heavily because public charitable donations had always been one way to buy a title.

The Commissioner had lowered the frequency of his meetings at Scotland Yard on the Tower case to weekly. There seemed to be nothing breaking. Superintendent Cooper had got the furthest, and his suspect, Captain Jackson, was still the only prospect. Surveillance on him was producing nothing. It was clear he would play it straight until it suited him to act. Privately the Commissioner confided that he thought Jackson was the man. Why? Because he had done it for family honor. Any man named Roderick Blood Jackson, with ties to the original Colonel Blood, had got to have a mission about it, hadn't he? We couldn't prove it, but we wouldn't give up.

The Commissioner explained to the next conference the fix he was in, "The problem is cost, gentlemen. The County forces' budgets have taken a beating and so has ours. The P.M. has made us some allowances from central funds but not enough. We're going to have to wind down our effort on the Tower job and only follow promising leads. I hate having to admit it, but until Jackson or someone else makes a move, our investigations have to be scaled down."

Rod made no attempt to contact Bill Harding or Mike Corder. They were doing exactly as they were told, nothing. They got on with their lives and watched developments through the media. Rod had a slight worry when the government announced a reward of £1 million for any information leading to the recovery of the Crown Jewels, no matter how slim the lead. It was the biggest reward ever offered in Britain. Mike Corder was dirt poor and might have gone for it. Then Rod realized that all Mike could do was betray his colleagues; he didn't know where the jewels were hidden so couldn't be the means of retrieving them. And anyway he wouldn't squeal on his Marine friends.

Superintendent Charles Creighton, the new Head of Thames Division, had ordered the damaged mooring pile to be replaced, and the pontoon lifted and checked for cracks and leaks. The piling had been done from the floating crane now moored there, and chains were fixed to the lifting points on the pontoon. The diesel fuel had been pumped out and she was riding high. As the pontoon rocked gently in the swell, and the lifting crew walked across it, it tilted and one corner came out of the water. A bright sun was shining at a low winter angle. Was it just imagination, or was there an occasional flash of something brilliant below the surface?

Superintendent Creighton disliked anyone from the Police's F1 Division because they were always bad news. F1 were the money men. They had oversight of all spending in the Metropolitan Police. No one liked them. They nagged continually about cost-effective use of resources, extension of compulsory outside competitive tendering for support services, activity sampling and costing, civilianisation of police jobs, and much more.

Now here was this fresh-faced young Inspector with an accounting degree in Creighton's office telling him he was badly over budget and must cut back.

"I must tell you, Superintendent, that the quotation you have submitted for this current work will cause you to lose one patrol launch next financial year."

The chains tightened outside as the engine on the crane barge began to increase power. The pontoon inched clear of the water. The lifting crew began to peer underneath, checking for weed and obstructions. One of them thought he saw something caught below the pontoon, some sort of sacking.

Creighton opened his window and shouted to the workmen, "Belay that lift! We're canceling the job. I'll be down in a minute to explain."

Creighton turned to the F1 Inspector, "Will that do? Lifting and renovating the pontoon was more than half the cost of the quotation."

The Inspector checked his figures, "Yes, that will probably do it, but I'll leave you with this list of cost-cutting measures, and I urge you, Sir, to try and implement them within the Division." He put the file on Creighton's desk.

"Yes, yes, thank you", said Creighton dismissively.

The Inspector took the hint and rose to go. Creighton walked outside to the pontoon, angry that his project had been canceled under him.

He told the barge crew, "Bloody budget restraints! The piling's done, we'll have to leave the tank for the next financial year."

The barge crew were not happy at having their work contract cut in half, and muttered about the Superintendent hearing from their boss.

Creighton turned away, unaware that he was only ten seconds from becoming the most famous policeman in Britain.

The public tends to forget sensational events quite quickly. Other things catch their imagination. Life in Britain went on, and on the surface things seemed back to normal. But the monarchy had taken a severe blow in public esteem, there was no doubt about that. There had always been a delicate love-hate relationship between the people and the whole idea of royalty. A philosopher had once observed that Britain might best be described as an infinity of republics. The monarchy was tolerated so long as it's members behaved themselves. They were there to set an example in all things.

The Queen was mostly admired for her dedication to a difficult job. But the rest of the large family were widely seen as expensive parasites, costing millions annually in tax-payers' money, and an enormous retinue of hangers-on fed on the whole royal apparatus. The Queen herself commonly referred to the royal family as 'The Firm'. The family's continuing petulance over the missing Crown Jewels soured this delicate balance between the public and the monarchy, and continued to do so. Rod watched all these developments carefully because his next step was something he couldn't do without great risk. He was looking for a signal, a sign, some indication that the time was right for him to cash in on his great hoard of treasure.

When the signal came it was a tiny thing, so small it was like a mustard seed. So apparently insignificant that no one would have guessed what it would lead to. It was a brief letter to The Times newspaper. It wasn't given any particular prominence. It was just an item on the letters page. It carried the heading:

'Stuart Heir Born On British Shore.'

The letter explained simply how the De Jure Head of the Royal House of Stuart, Albert, Duke of Bavaria, was still living in Europe, and that to his family a son had been born. The parents had come to Britain for the birth so the boy could eventually claim his rightful inheritance.

As the letter said, 'The royal baby born in London to the Crown Prince and Princess will be eventually the Head of the Royal House of Stuart.'

Some odd things began to happen. Other newspapers picked it up and used it in part or in full. But as the general public might have some problems with the Latin phrase 'De Jure' it was explained.

The translation was, 'By Right, From The Law.'

And that was it, the seed, the spark. All that followed grew from there.

These phrases 'De Jure' and 'By Right, From The Law' somehow took root in the national consciousness. And there was such a thing. People awoke to a new understanding they didn't have before. Previously the choice on the question of the monarchy had been too stark. Either to have one or not. And the pro-monarchy lobby had played skillfully on the fear of what might fill the void if the monarchy disappeared. But now people realized it was possible to have the best of both worlds. Those traditionalists who felt a monarchy must stay at all costs would be satisfied because the Stuart Royal House clearly had a more ancient and rightful claim than the House of Windsor.

As the guide books sold in the Tower of London itself made absolutely clear, 'But for the Act of Settlement the present King of Great Britain is Duke Albert of Bavaria. The 1701 Act of Succession was passed to bar from the royal succession any member of the royal family who married a Catholic.'

Also all those who were dissatisfied with the monarchy because of the Windsors' high-handed conduct and great expense would be satisfied too, because waiting in the wings was a better alternative, and not a bogus one but the rightful one, the Stuarts. It all made sense.

School history lessons had left a residue of knowledge in the nation about Bonnie Prince Charlie and his brave attempt in 1745 to regain the throne for the Royal House of Stuart. Indeed, Hollywood had made films about it. These highlighted how England's Hanoverian King, the German George II, was running scared and about to leave London as Prince Charles Stuart reached Derby, only 100 miles away; and the great cruelties done to the Scots at Culloden in 1746, with the murdering of their wounded and the smashing of the clans. Whatever the facts of the case, it was the romanticized version which caught the public's imagination.

The tabloid press, always willing to knock the establishment, was the first to voice openly this new public feeling of support for the Stuarts and dislike of the Windsors. The serious newspapers took up the theme in leading articles, and television commentaries and debates followed. The polls on the issue of a monarchy had been fairly evenly divided. Now people were saying, well Britain had always been a monarchy so it might be nice if it could stay that way, but wouldn't it be better if the Royal House of Stuart was called back. After all, their De Jure rights preceded the Windsors' by a long way. De Jure had become a common and popular phrase.

The movement grew and it didn't go away. The once forbidden loyal toast to the Stuart Royal House became fashionable. Wine glasses were passed over a glass of water to the words, "The King over the water", meaning the real King living abroad across the English Channel.

The Palace had to take notice of all of this and didn't like it. Their media machine wanted to act but could do nothing about it. To mention the problem publicly was to acknowledge that it existed. And to do so was to admit that it was a cause of serious concern. The reality was that it was too late to rescue the collective reputation of the Windsors from their many moral scandals over the years. They had long ceased to have the respect of the majority of the people.

Another article in The Times pointed out that in England at the time of the Reformation in the 1500's, King Henry VIII had published a treatise defending the true Catholic faith against the German Protestant Luther. A grateful Pope had rewarded Henry with the title 'Fidei Defensor', Defender of the Faith. The Windsors still dared to use it on their coins as 'Fid Def' or 'F.D.' But a family deeply prone to divorce, sexual affairs and low moral conduct was hardly qualified to retain the title. No one claimed the Stuarts would be any better, but they could hardly be any worse. And they would at least be a modern

European style monarchy, accessible, friendly and sensitive to the lives of all the people, not just the rich and remote upper classes.

Rod watched all these developments with fascination. It had happened much sooner than he hoped. He thought it might take about a year. It had taken only about six months. He began to plan his final move. He had to time it exactly right.

Professor Carbery's article in 'Nature' caused a big stir, as he had hoped it would. The more publicity the better from his point of view. It might lead to a television debate with him in the starring role. And so it did.

Superintendent Cooper was bored at home, as he often was. He and his wife had no children and shared no interests. As a friend had put it, they went together like Teflon and Velcro.

His main interest was motorcycling, about which he was passionate. He had a fast bike and rode to all the race meetings he could. He had also toured all over Europe by motorbike. She wouldn't go on any of his bikes and hated them. Her big passion was bridge, which she played several times a week. He thought that a boring waste of time. There was little on television worth watching. He was trawling the channels when a brainy looking man came on, talking animatedly,

"Yes, extraordinary, the algae Stigeoclonium Mumbaii growing on vessels in the North Sea. It was indeed specific only to Bombay Harbor but grows now along the Suffolk coast and possibly elsewhere. I have myself taken specimens from a fishing boat in Lowestoft harbor."

Cooper didn't hear the rest, he was on the phone, "Get onto BBC2 at once and find out who that is on now going on about stuff on fishing boats in the North Sea. I must have his name, address and phone number without fail, and I mean without fail! Call me back at home."

Meanwhile his wife had switched channels! "Well you weren't really watching, and I want my program, you did say I could have it."

She pouted as he fumed and tried to regain BBC2. By the time he had, the credits were rolling.

The return call gave him Carbery's name and details. Cooper gave rapid orders to his assistant, "Right, get onto Oxford police, their top man. Get him to send someone round tonight and to wait till Carbery gets there. Tell Carbery to keep himself available at ten tomorrow. I'll see him then. If he has appointments, and he will, insist he cancels them. If he won't play ball, tell him it's of the utmost urgency but don't tell him why. Got it? OK, be in my office by seven tomorrow. Yes, seven."

"Anything interesting? ", asked his wife.

"No, not really; I'll be off a bit early in the morning."

"Oh not again", she said in a whining voice, "You've hardly spent any time at home in these last few months. Mother wants you to take her to see Aunt Madge. You know they both love to see you."

The next morning a policeman stood on duty at the gates to Logic Lane off Oxford's High Street. Cooper's police car pulled in early at 9.45. The Master's Lodgings faced Logic Lane, and the Master's Secretary, Elizabeth Rowles, admitted Cooper to the large hall with it's imposing staircase.

Rowles said coolly, "The Master will see you at ten", and motioned Cooper to a chair.

The study was on the first floor and at 10.05 Miss Rowles led Cooper up, knocked and entered, "Superintendent Cooper for you, Master."

Carbery looked older in the flesh than he had on television; perhaps it was the make-up and flattering lighting. He exuded a nervous intelligence. A bachelor like so many academics, his work was his life.

He probably didn't mean to be condescending to Cooper but that's how it came out, "How can I help you, Superintendent? I'm sure this must be important or you wouldn't be here. I was bidden to stay by the Chief Constable, no less. Sadly I can hardly tell the Fellows my absence from their meeting is because I am helping the police with their inquiries." He laughed lightly at his own joke.

Cooper was not going to play the plodder to this genius, "It's about your television appearance last night, Sir, and your article in 'Nature'. I read it coming up in the car."

It was a good riposte not lost on Carbery. The article he considered so important was light reading for a car trip. He raised an eyebrow. Why on earth should the police, and senior police at that, take such an interest in his work?

He said, "I'm pleased you've seen it, Superintendent, but how can it be relevant to your work?"

"You say, Sir, that the growth you took off a boat in Lowestoft harbor is specific only to Bombay?"

"Oh yes, quite so, or it was till I showed otherwise. You see Bombay has had it's enormous slums for a very long time. The Chadwick Report of 1832 dealt with cholera and it's causes in the slums of Britain. The report refers to Glasgow as second only to Bombay as the filthiest city in the British Empire. So there has been plenty of time for the cocktail of nutrients which grace Bombay's harbor to grow it's own species of algae. Mumbai means Bombay in Hindi."

Carbery was just getting warmed up. Cooper felt like being back in a university tutorial. Carbery went on, "Fauna as well as flora can be narrowly specific; look at the sparrow unique to the tiny island of St. Kilda; Sydney harbor has it's own species of shark; the Galapagos it's inhabitants, and so on."

He paused and that gave Cooper his chance, "Our interest lies in the boat from which you took your samples, Sir. Have you any notes about the boat, time and place?"

"Oh yes, I keep accurate notes, they are the basis of my work. Now, where did I put them? Ah, my vacation pocket book is in my bedroom, I'll just go and get it."

The wait seemed interminable. It was probably two minutes, "Yes, here we are. Lowestoft Quay, scraped several samples of Stigeoclonium Mumbaii from the lower left rear hull of a fishing vessel called Theseus."

Cooper sighed with deep satisfaction, "Aaaah!", then added slowly, "Professor, you are about to become the most famous scientist in Britain, but not for the reason you might think."

"How extraordinary! What do you mean?"

"I mean, Professor, that you have probably helped us solve a most important case."

"Well I'm so glad. Is there anything else?"

"Yes please, could you ask your secretary to make a copy for us of the page you have just read?"

"Certainly, it will only take a minute", and he pressed a bell and the job was done.

Cooper took his leave, and unusually for him, shook hands. He said firmly, "Thank you very much indeed, Professor."

A sudden look of understanding came into Carbery's eyes, "You don't mean that case, do you?" Cooper nodded and Carbery gasped, "My God! I will be famous!"

In the car outside Cooper ordered the driver to, "Drive like hell to Lowestoft! And don't worry about speeding, use your lights and siren when you have to."

The driver grinned and floored it. He was looking forward to 150 miles of flat-out cross-country work. A Class 1 driver, there was none more skillful, and the car spent much of the trip at well over 100 mph. Cooper called ahead to the Suffolk County Police Headquarters at Martlesham Heath near Ipswich. He got clearance to take all the police in the Lowestoft area off their current duty and to cordon off the docks. They were to await his arrival and no one was to leave. They wouldn't like it as they'd been bothered twice before, but they'd have to put up with it. Dock workers trying to go home for lunch found their way barred.

The police tried to explain, "Sorry, Sir, won't keep you long. Some urgent inquiries are in progress and we need your help."

"Aw, not the friggin' Theseus again, is it? We've been all over that. She's buggered off, ain't she? Haven't you coppers understood that yet?"

The docks were large and Cooper gave orders for all the people inside the extensive cordon to be herded to an open warehouse and stood in line. He sat on a crate as the dock workers filed past.

The general tenor of the grumbling was, "Yeah, like I told them coppers before, we all seen the Theseus, she was here about fifteen years, along with all the others. Then the friggin' Common Market cut the fishing quotas so the boats couldn't make a living and she got sold off."

To the query, "When did you last see her?", came the usual exasperated response, "Nah, how should I know? Sometime last Spring I should fink, can't do better than that."

The long line had nearly all gone through and no new details had come to light. Cooper was losing heart. It looked like a lost cause.

Three from the end he came to Bert Johnson, "Yeah, I know her, my men worked on her."

Cooper's spirits rose at once, "Excellent, when was that?"

"Can't say till I look at me books. We had two or three small jobs at the same time. You'll have to come to the office."

The few men left were asked to wait while Cooper followed Johnson. The waiting men continued their grousing,

"Never known such a friggin' fuss about a few drugs."

"Nah, it ain't drugs, mate. They wouldn't make all this fuss over a bit of drugs. I reckon it's the IRA and guns or summat like that."

"Sod the lot of 'em! I want me friggin' grub! My missus won't half give me stick when I get in, she'll swear I've been down the pub again."

In the small cluttered office of Bert Johnson a search through the jobs book found the entry.

Bert said, "There we are, Theseus, in then, out then, paid cash."

"Thank you, we need to find her urgently. Can you give us any clues where she might be?"

"No mate. You won't find her, at least not like that."

"Why not?", asked Cooper.

Bert reached up to a cork pinboard and pulled down a photo, "Because he re-named her after my little girl, didn't he."

Cooper nearly danced round the office, "Got him! Got him at last! We've caught him in a lie. It proves he had something to hide."

Then more calmly, "May I keep the photo and book for a while? I'll give you a receipt and you'll get them back. I'll need your full name, address and phone number. You might be called as a witness."

"Sure, anything I can do to help", said Bert.

Cooper thanked the local police, dismissed the remaining men and drove back to London. He was jubilant. This could sew it up. He got through to London and gave orders for the port search to be started again, beginning with King's Lynn and working up and down the coast from there. It would take a while to trace the Crystal but he'd get there in the end.

It took two days to get the report from the Hull police, "Yes, cut up by Humber Breakers Ltd. Sold by a man called Jackson for cash. Yes, we've seen the books and taken a statement. It's genuine alright. We can bring the yard owner down if you like."

"No, that won't be necessary thanks."

At Scotland Yard the Commissioner sat in on the meeting called to review the evidence against Jackson. Cooper set out the details as he saw them.

"We have a man with an odd name, related to the person who made the last nearly successful attempt on the Crown Jewels. A possible motive but not one a court would accept. He's an ex-Royal Marine Commando Captain, chosen for the Special Boat Service, and therefore certainly a very able swimmer. Our surveillance on him shows he swims almost daily. He could easily do the job but that's not evidence he did it. He was on the last training course for capital ships, so he could work the Belfast's guns, or he and a colleague could. We know from Navy records that Maclean served on the Belfast, so he has worked in X-Turret on her, but we can't tie them to the ship."

Cooper paused briefly, "Jackson's boat was in St. Katherine's Dock before, during and after the event. We know he was there and that puts him close to the Belfast and the Tower. But his alibi seems rock solid. At least ten people have sworn he was on the Galatea all night, and he was in fact the host. He made love to at least one of the women there, and one claims he slept with her for most of the night."

Cooper smiled, "She seemed rather pleased that her own prowess had put him into a deep sleep and they didn't wake till late morning."

Some in the audience chuckled at the implied sexual athleticism. Some of the few women in the room shifted in their seats, crossing their legs.

Cooper went on, "Maclean was home at his pub in Suffolk, so his wife says, upstairs feeling ill, and later inquiries do show that he has been unwell and slow to recover. The Tower guards reported seeing four men, and

138

the other two have never been found. It's a great pity the airport lead fizzled out because clearly he was a fifth helper. The fireworks display was a diversion we haven't solved, and the white BMW was clearly a decoy run. Jackson's car tire contained two pieces of typeface, one of which looks like that on the decoy letters, but we can't tie him to the letters, there were no prints on them."

He looked round the audience meaningfully, "It gets a bit better now. He takes his boat out of the Thames, changes it's name and sells it to a breakers so it will never be found. So he's got something to hide, and he lied at this point. He said he'd sold his boat to a Larsen in King's Lynn. But lying to the police is not an indictable offense, as we know it goes on all the time. We think the shells used in the Belfast were those stolen from near Bombay. We can't prove this yet, but the Kashmir slogan was a blind, as the shells have never turned up in India. Can we prove that Jackson's boat was in Bombay? If we can, the circle of evidence round him begins to tighten to the point where we might get a judge and jury to believe it."

Cooper summed up with emphasis, "To do this we have to break the reputation of Britain's most eminent marine biologist. He has just staked it on his claim that the weed he found on Jackson's boat, and which grows only in Bombay harbor, is now growing in the warming North Sea."

There was a long silence as the audience took it all in. They waited for the Commissioner to speak first. He said simply, "Comments please?"

There was another long pause while people tried to think of something plausible to say. One said hopefully, "We could hold him on suspicion, try and rattle him, then offer him a deal in return for the jewels."

Cooper replied, "It would be unlikely to work. These people get training in anti-interrogation techniques much tougher than anything we practice."

Again no one wanted to speak, so the Commissioner summed up, "A court won't convict on what we've got now. If we go in too soon and there's an acquittal, Jackson would be a hero and we don't want that."

Turning to Cooper, the Commissioner added, "Thank you, Superintendent, for your good work so far. As discreetly as you can, interview all those academics who oppose Carbery's views and collate their responses. Video them if they agree, if not, at least tape them. We must have a body of expert opinion to outweigh and discredit him. It will take some time but press on with it as quickly as you can."

CHAPTER 8: REWARD.

Rod judged the moment right to make his final move. Driving into Ipswich he bought a cheap portable typewriter, paper and envelopes. If he was watched, it wasn't important. His yacht he kept in the water all year round except for an annual anti-fouling treatment. He often enjoyed early Spring or late Fall trips on the river or out to sea. The days were crisp and clear, and often he had the area to himself.

He packed a lunch, and with the typewriter in the same bag, rowed out to his boat, slipped the mooring and motored downriver. In the estuary he raised the sails and headed out to sea. Several miles out he set the tiller and went below. Using thin plastic gloves he typed two letters and addressed their envelopes. The typewriter, spare paper and envelopes went into the empty lunch bag. Back on deck he let the bag slip over the side. It went down in fifty feet of water. He put the tiller over and headed back to the mouth of the River Deben, being careful as always over the tricky shingle bar at the entrance.

Professor Carbery's views on certain aspects of marine biology were opposed by many of his contemporaries. He was not popular with them because he was too popular with the public. His publicity seeking ways had caused some jealousy. His opponents regarded themselves as more rigorous in their work, and more scrupulous in their approach to publishing. They would only publish when their work was proven, not mere theories. No less than five leading authorities were willing to testify that in their expert opinion Carbery was wrong about the Stigeoclonium Mumbaii. In fact they implied they would rather enjoy cutting him down to size.

Cooper went to interview them all and this took time. One was in North Wales, and one was at St. Andrew's University in Scotland. He was a Dr. Rupert Craggs, and his work on algae was as well regarded as that of Professor Carbery. Cooper completed these visits within a week, then sought permission from the Commissioner to take the file on Jackson to the Office of the Director of Public Prosecutions for a formal opinion. The Commissioner insisted that the Director herself, the brilliant Dr. Angela Wheatcroft, dealt with the case. Wheatcroft told Cooper she would need the file for twenty four hours and would call back.

When she did, she was direct, "None of the material here would in itself lead to a conviction. But taken together as a body of evidence it makes an impressive indictment. As you know, clever counsel can sway juries, so a conviction might be possible. I would rate the chances as fifty-fifty. But my advice would be not to proceed at this stage for one simple reason. Even with as much jury-rigging as the government might feel it could get away with, in this current atmosphere I don't think you could assemble a jury which would convict Jackson without incontrovertible proof. You've got nearly enough here, Superintendent, but not quite. You need one more solid piece to form the keystone of your arch."

Cooper was stoical, "Thank you, Dr. Wheatcroft, I thought as much. We'll have to keep digging. We'll get there in the end."

Crank letters of all kinds came in steadily to Scotland Yard, each trying for a piece of the £1 million reward. All were followed up with care and zeal to see if they made any sense. None had yet. It was Cooper's job, along with others, to assess these letters. They sat round a large table and studied the three in that morning. Cooper opened them in turn. The first was from a medium who claimed she had seen in a dream that the jewels were behind King Arthur's Round Table hung on the wall in

Winchester Cathedral. The second said he'd seen something flashing that looked like a crown on the sea bed between the island of Mull and the holy island of Iona.

It was the third letter which brought Cooper up with a start. He read it then said in a voice which told everyone instantly how important it was, "This is genuine. We are being offered a deal to get the jewels back. I'm going to see the Commissioner", and he was out of his chair before the others got a chance to see what was in the letter.

The Commissioner had learned to set aside what he was doing when Cooper asked to be seen.

The secretary was dismissed in mid-sentence and Cooper went in, "This came into 10 Downing Street this morning, Sir. No prints."

Cooper handed over the note and the Commissioner read it out aloud.

"Prime Minister, the time has come for the regalia to be returned, under certain conditions. These are:

1. A full pardon for the four participants, to be signed by H.M. The Queen, the Lord Chief Justice, and you.
2. No names to be published, ever.
3. A payment of £5 million to each participant. Note that this is a tiny fraction of the jewels' worth.
4. The Act of Succession to be repealed within the next session of Parliament, and a public promise on this made in the media within one week from today.
5. The regalia will be returned intact, but it is an absolute condition that the Stuart Sapphire be removed from the Imperial State Crown and given into the possession of the writer without further claim by the State or Crown in perpetuity.
6. A means has been devised whereby the regalia will appear to be recovered by the police. Choose a long-serving diver, close to retirement, with a big family, and deserving of the £1 million reward. Confirm that he will

143

receive it. Superintendent Cooper to be promoted to Commander and this confirmed in public. These means will allow the government to appear successful in their efforts to recover the regalia.

7. You have one week to comply in full. Failure to comply will cause the regalia to be broken up and dispersed abroad.

8. To comply, place this notice in The Times:
Ariadne, points 1 to 7 are agreed in full.' You will then receive a further communication."

The Commissioner, missing the main point, said, "So that's it, it's a ransom job. What makes you think it's genuine?"

Cooper replied, "Jackson can't sign it, Sir, it would tie him to the letter. But he has to tell us it's genuine so we'll believe it. He needs a code word we'll understand, or some of us will, so he uses the name Ariadne."

The point was not lost on the Commissioner. He said tartly, "Pardon my ignorance, Cooper, but why should Ariadne mean Jackson sent this?"

"His boat was called the Theseus, Sir. In Greek legend Ariadne gave Theseus a clue of thread to guide him out of the labyrinth. He's bit of a joker our man Jackson, but I'll stake my promotion on it." Cooper allowed himself a smile.

The Commissioner gave him a hard, quizzical stare, "You wouldn't be in league with this man, would you, Cooper?"

"No Sir, but we need to move fast to get these points seen to. I imagine the P.M. will be the first port of call, then he'll tell the Palace?"

"Right", said the Commissioner, "I want you with me on this. If it's a hoax we'll go down together."

They were lucky to catch the P.M. He was due to leave for Brussels at midday. He canceled over the protests of his Private Secretary, "But Prime Minister you're due to give the keynote speech there this evening."

144

"Then the Foreign Secretary will have to do it. Get him for me now."

The P.M. was convinced by Cooper's reasoning on the ransom note and said, quite wrongly, "I think we have forced this person to show his hand. I will consult the Cabinet on each of the items here, and then will have to put it to Her Majesty. In my view she would be wise to accept. But we'll have to see. Thank you, gentlemen.

The Cabinet met within the hour, and as might be expected of twenty two politicians, they were divided on the terms.

The P.M. made it clear in his opening statement that the conditions were much better than they could have hoped for, "Clearly the man is not a common thief. If he were the jewels would have been out of the country and broken up long ago. We would never have found them. I must add that the terms save all our faces. It will probably guarantee our re-election. The only sticking point, as far as I can see, is persuading Her Majesty to repeal the Act of Succession. As you know, repeal would allow monarchs to marry Catholics and for them to ascend the throne."

Turning to John Plummer, the Minister for Transport, the P.M. added, "I imagine, John, repeal of the Act has your full support?"

"Indeed so, Prime Minister", smiled the Catholic member of the Cabinet, "But not perhaps for the reason you might imagine. When the Act was framed centuries ago there was deep religious prejudice. Surely we are above that now? Just as there is freedom of choice in politics, so there is freedom of worship for the people. The monarch rules under the law, not above the law. And Parliament makes the laws. Her Majesty would not dare to oppose a Bill we pass. Victoria in 1839 was the last to try, and she was forced to back down. I say we don't ask Her Majesty if we can do this thing, we say our will is firm on the matter and present it as agreed in Cabinet."

It was a clever move to switch deftly from a merely pro-Catholic argument to a stance they could all support. There were nods of assent all round the big oval table.

Mrs. Mortimer, for Education, and a Baptist, interjected, "The Free Churches won't like it, and the Church of England might oppose it."

The P.M. was cutting, "The Free Churches comprise, I suspect, less than one percent of the population, and Canterbury and his bishops seem to me half way to Rome already. I must say I almost look forward to witnessing the near apoplexy of the Reverend Dr. Liam Gazeley."

There was a chuckle of laughter round the room as the P.M. concluded, "Thank you, we seem agreed. I will ask Her Majesty for an audience."

Rod made no special effort to go out and buy The Times, it was delivered daily to his house. He scanned it much more carefully than usual. His wife noticed, as they do, "You seem absorbed in the paper these days. I do wish you'd see to that garden fence. The dog has got out twice this week already. Mrs. Watson's bitch is in season and poor Jake is after her."

"He'll get a bloody hernia if he tries. Have you seen a spaniel try it on with a labrador?"

"Don't be vulgar, dear."

The Prime Minister had emphasized the urgency of the request for an audience at the Palace, saying they were close to regaining the regalia. The Queen was visibly warmer when he entered and bowed, and she motioned him to a chair. He had planned to leave till last the point about changing the Act of Succession. He went through the points one by one. She did not demur at the pardons, though she said she disliked the idea of the perpetrators going free after causing so much damage.

Even the idea of losing the Stuart Sapphire seemed not too distressful. After all, she thought it's value slight compared to the great diamonds. In mere money terms she was right, but she failed to discern it's real political importance.

She said disdainfully, "So he's a Jacobite and a supporter of the Stuarts, is he? Much good may it do him. I feel the House of Windsor is well enough established, don't you, Prime Minister?"

Their eyes met and she knew instantly that he disagreed completely. He lied unconvincingly, "Yes, Ma'am."

He came then to the point about the Repeal of the Act of Succession.

Her face clouded over and she said icily, "This is too much!"

He tried to placate her, "It is no immediate threat to your House, Ma'am. It does seem to right an oddity in our laws. No other monarchy has such a provision."

"Damn the others! We took an oath at our coronation to maintain the laws, rights and privileges of the Crown. This demand makes a chink in our armor which could become a yawning gap in time."

Urging common sense, he said, "Ma'am, I must point out that we now have less than a week in which to concur or you lose your regalia for ever."

She was unmoved, "Changing the constitution under duress is a despicable thing, Prime Minister. We shall take advice on this", and she rose to go.

He wasn't going to let her get away with that. She had been troublesome for months while he'd sweated to recover the jewels. It was time to tell her plainly where she stood.

Rising too, he said bluntly, "Ma'am, it is your duly elected Ministers who by long custom are your advisers, and I must inform you that the Cabinet feels it would be wise to accept the terms, unpalatable though they might be."

She rounded on him fiercely, "So you have decided, have you? Well, we have our own sources of advice and we will consult them!", and she swept out of the room.

147

"Damn!", he cursed quietly. She could spoil the whole plan. If she withheld her signature from the pardons, Jackson would not go through with his promise to return the regalia.

The next few days were increasingly tense. The Queen called together her whole family, with her most trusted adviser, Lord Steven St. John. He was a constitutional expert, and convinced entirely in his own mind that a monarchy was the best institution to lead British life. What he understood very well, but the Queen and her family didn't, was that it was the institution he cherished, not the present holders of it. Privately he thought the Windsors surpassingly dull in all respects, and deeply immoral to the core. The Queen and her family, so used to fawning hangers-on, were simply unable to discern that Lord St. John's arguments in support of the monarchy were for a splendid and charismatic leadership, full of style and above suspicion. The Windsors had shown time and again that they could never achieve this, but until something better came along they would have to do. Besides, he liked the social status he gained from rubbing elbows with the royals. So he dissembled brilliantly, knowing his audience hadn't the wit to penetrate his real views.

Each person present was invited in turn to give their opinions on Jackson's proposals, and did so. Lord St. John spoke with eloquent persuasiveness, "In essence, Ma'am, little will change. Repealing the Act has no immediate effect at all, it merely gives your heirs more freedom of choice in the future. We should not fear this, but welcome it. I am, as you know, a loyal supporter of the monarchy, and I would not make any recommendation which might damage it. I have argued on television that for the monarchy to flourish it should be seen to be a grand and regal one, and on balance the return of your regalia will enable this to be so once again."

The Queen had listened attentively; she respected the man's views. She summed up by turning to Prince

Charles, "Charles, the last word must come from you. I am little affected by all this, but you might re-marry and much could hang on your choice."

Charles' brow furrowed in deep thought, and he spoke hesitantly, "It's the principles in life which matter, not the quibbling over minor details. So Anglican or Catholic isn't really important, they're both just branches of the same faith. If all this man wants is a pardon and a law which allows that a Catholic might reign in the future, I see no objection at all."

She summed up, "Thank you, Charles. We seem agreed then. We will give the man what he wants in return for the regalia." Then with a cruel attempt at humor, "I suppose I should tell the P.M. and put the poor man out if his misery."

They all laughed dutifully.

The P.M. put the phone down, "Thank God for that! She's agreed. Get that notice round to The Times right away. She's cut it damned fine."

Rod had been getting anxious about the late appearance of the reply to his demands. It came on the last day he had allowed. He drove into Ipswich and parked, and walked to the main post office. Looking at the collection times, he waited till the next one and posted his letter just in time to catch it.

Although events were rolling towards a deal with Jackson, the idea of having to give in to him stuck in the throat of the Commissioner. His police force didn't look good. He determined to have one last go at finding the jewels. In Jackson's list of demands he had asked for a diver, so the jewels were in the river somewhere, but where? They had to be downstream of the Tower because the tide was running out strongly as the raid ended. But they could be anywhere between the Tower and the Thames Barrier, or even beyond. It was an impossible job to search all those miles. But just in case the jewels were anchored on the river bed near the Tower, a team of police divers was set to work there.

Nothing was found. The tide scoured strongly there as it funneled through the narrow arches of Tower bridge. One diver saw a piece of scrap metal sticking out of the gravel but ignored it and swam on. It was a rusting sword blade. Tiny traces of blood remained in the grain sealed under the rust.

Cooper's mind continued to churn away on the case. He couldn't turn it off. It was like an engine running on it's own. It was time for some fundamental thinking. What was wrong with the police approach to the case? They were going about it like policemen. They weren't going about it like the raiders. And who were they? They were ex-Marine Commandos, and not just ordinary ones, but members of the Special Boat Service. What special skill must they have, apart from all the others, to become a member of the S.B.S? They had to be brilliant swimmers.

Following this general idea, but with no particular plan in mind, Cooper had a police launch put at his disposal. He went to Wapping Police Station and boarded it. The pontoon rocked slightly as he crossed it. He gave orders to go up to the Tower of London, then slowly all the way down to the Thames Barrier.

It was a sunny day and he enjoyed the boat ride. It was confusing though, there were so many good hiding places the task of finding the one that mattered was simply impossible. If the jewels were anywhere connected with the river they could be on a boat and long gone from the stretch between the Tower and Barrier. The case seemed hopeless, impossible of solution. The launch ended it's trip and returned Cooper to the pontoon at Wapping. He disembarked and decided to walk for a while.

He turned left into Wapping High Street, and took the first opportunity to join the footpath which ran along the river bank. Coming to a bench, he sat on it and stared idly downriver. The police boats were busily coming and going from the pontoon. He nearly dozed off.

The mind though was still ticking away, like a watch never stops. What about this man Jackson? We can't find the jewels, but what can we find out from the man? What was he really like? What quality did he have which we've overlooked?

Anyone watching Cooper at that moment might have thought he was an epileptic. His body began to convulse and then heave up and down. Then he could contain it no longer. He roared out loud with laughter.

"Of course! Of course! A sense of humor! The man's a bloody joker!"

Then another outburst of laughing, before, "They're under the pontoon! They've got to be under the pontoon. Where else could they be? It's always crawling with cops. What a bloody joker!"

He got up and walked slowly away, still chuckling to himself.

The announcement that the 1701 Act of Succession was to be repealed had been hidden in print as small as possible on an inner page of The Times. The P.M's Private Secretary had virtually begged the editor not to make a major news item out of it. But it still caused an uproar in Protestant circles, specially in Northern Ireland where it was denounced as, 'caving in to pressure from Eire'. True to form, the Rev. Dr. Liam Gazeley foamed and ranted about the 'treacherous government' and the 'return to Rome', and how this could only strengthen the hand of the IRA who would see it as yet another sign of weakness. He was always good television value for these verbal fireworks, but only briefly because he was essentially boring in his predictability.

The leader writers in the serious press dealt with the topic of repealing the Act of Succession according to their paymasters' wishes, but most could see no objection to it. It was a step towards modernity, the removal of an outdated and unjust law based on religious prejudice in centuries past. The tabloids made a coarser meal of it:

'Charles Can Marry A Catholic!'
'OK For Prince William And Harry To Date Catholic Girls!'

There was a great deal of early match-making with the eligible Catholic Princesses of Europe. Naturally the papers showed pictures of the pretty ones, and claimed they were more beautiful and better born than the Protestant ones.

Around Britain though, many people saw the real importance of the reforms, and began to voice it. That it was the beginning of the end for the Windsors.

The second letter which Rod had typed on his boat he had addressed directly to the Police Commissioner:

'One week from today take the following action:

1. Assemble at 10 a.m. the Prime Minister, yourself and Commander Cooper at Wapping Police Station. Have there your chosen diver. I will ask his name.
2. Bring four pardons, signed as instructed, with spaces for the names to be inserted.
3. Bring four bank statements from the Royal Bank of Jersey showing that £5 million has been deposited in

each account. The accounts are to be named Mr. A, B, C and D. The bank to be told that these accounts are the property of four people who will arrive and identify themselves by producing the statements. Their names will be given then.

4. Bring an Affidavit, legally binding, signed by the Prime Minister and yourself, that the Stuart Sapphire will be delivered to me within one week of the return of the Crown Jewels.

5. Any attempt to arrest me, or failure to comply with all these points, will lead to the immediate release to the media of the full text of both these letters. Ariadne.'

The announcement within the Metropolitan Police of Cooper's promotion to Commander had been kept to a very small circle. He held the rank and pay but it was not to become widely known till after the return of the regalia. Cooper had agreed to this. He and the Commissioner took Jackson's letter to the Prime Minister, and a small team set about fulfilling it's requirements.

The P.M's reaction was understandable, "I don't want to be seen doing this, Commissioner. Arrange a car for me with darkened windows so I can go to and fro unseen. It should be a secure one too if it's to carry the Crown Jewels."

"Certainly, Prime Minister, I will arrange that. My office will work with your Private Secretary on the details."

"Thank you, Commissioner. I must say I'm rather looking forward to it all. I haven't done any of this cloak and dagger stuff before." He rubbed his hands together like a schoolboy about to get a new bike.

The night before the big hand-over Rod stayed in a good hotel in London. He dined well and wined well. He was in good spirits and looking forward to the next day. He slept dreamlessly and awoke refreshed. A taxi dropped him at Wapping Police Station at 9.55 a.m. If he had been followed, and he had, he wasn't aware of it.

Superintendent Creighton was overjoyed and panic-stricken at the same time. The 'headless chicken' syndrome had gripped him with a vengeance. He had been told to stand by from 9.30 a.m. to receive high grade V.I.P's but had no idea whom. He had ordered an immediate clean-up of the station, to the extreme annoyance of the staff who couldn't get on with their work. And then for the Commissioner and the Prime Minister to walk in was almost too much. The veneer of his composure cracked and he began to babble inanely about the Division's performance being within budget limitations, and how well they all did despite these constraints. That was what they wanted to hear, wasn't it?

Jackson gave his real name and was shown into Creighton's office where the Commissioner and the P.M. were waiting. Each eyed the other cautiously. No one attempted to shake hands. The silence seemed long but was only a few seconds.

Rod said calmly, "Please ask this person to leave", and indicated Creighton.

The Commissioner nodded and Creighton sidled out like a crab.

Rod said, "You have the pardons?"

The Commissioner took them from a briefcase and put them on the table. Rod studied the wording and signatures, "Write in these names please", he said, handing over a slip of paper. The Commissioner wrote in the names.

Rod said, "The four bank statements please", and they were inspected.

Then Rod said, "The Affidavit on the Stuart Sapphire please", and this too was examined.

Satisfied, Rod put all the papers in his own tough alloy case, locked it, and locked it to his left wrist by the chain in his sleeve which went up his arm and round his waist. He motioned them to follow, and with puzzled looks they went outside and down the long gangway onto the pontoon. Two police boats were tied up there, and Rod saw at once that both contained armed men. Momentary fear of a trap gripped him but he controlled it at once.

Standing to one side was a middle aged but fit looking man dressed in full diving gear. His eyes widened when he saw who came onto the pontoon.

Rod walked over to him and shook hands, "Hallo, who are you?"

"Sergeant Morrison, Sir."

Rod said, "I understand you have a large family, Sergeant?"

"Yessir, seven children, three boys and four girls", he said proudly.

"Well done, Sergeant, but four weddings will be a bit of a strain on the pocket, won't it?"

"Oh we'll manage, Sir, we always do."

"Well good luck, Sergeant Morrison, I'm pleased to have met you. I was a diver myself a long time ago."

The P.M. was becoming impatient at this affable chat and demanded, "Well? Where are they?"

"You're standing on them."

"What?!"

"They're fixed under this pontoon and always have been. Send your diver down. He'll need bolt cutters."

The Commissioner called over Sergeant Morrison and told him to bring up whatever might be fixed to the underside of the pontoon, and to take very great care doing it. Morrison inserted his mouthpiece, checked his air supply, and descended the hand-grips built into the rear of the pontoon.

In the few minutes which followed, no one wanted to be the first to speak. The Commissioner broke first. He said to Rod disdainfully, "Your ransom demand wasn't much compared to the value of the jewels. Surely you could have got more for them on the open market?"

Rod gave him a withering look which conveyed quite clearly that Rod thought him an ill-informed half-wit. Turning to Cooper, Rod said, "You haven't explained to him then, Commander?"

Cooper, doing his best not to sound condescending, spoke gently to the Commissioner, "Ransom is not really the main aim of this operation, Sir. It is to put the Royal House of Stuart back on the throne. It won't happen soon, probably not in our lifetimes, but the way has been paved for it."

A look of slow understanding dawned on the Commissioner's face, "So that's it! Ah, thank you Superintendent, er, I mean Commander."

The diver's head reappeared and he emerged carrying the steel mesh sack. Stuck to it was weed, pieces of plastic, small bits of wood, paper and other rubbish. It looked completely worthless. He laid it between them.

Slightly tremulously the Commissioner said, "Cut it open very carefully, Sergeant."

The bolt cutters cropped each of the three steel cables in turn. He pulled them through the steel mesh and took out the interior nylon sack. This he opened very carefully.

The flashing of the huge diamonds was almost unbelievably bright.

"Cor! Bloody 'ell!", exclaimed the Sergeant.

The rest stood in silence, awed by the sight of the world's most magnificent jewels.

Rod said cheerfully, "Well done, Sergeant. The million pound reward is yours for finding the Crown Jewels. Isn't that so, Prime Minister?"

The P.M. jumped, "Er, yes indeed, well done, Sergeant."

"Cor! Bloody 'ell! And me retiring in a month's time. Wait till I tell the missus!"

The crowns had been buckled slightly by the weight of the pontoon, and the ivory rods of the scepters were snapped, but luckily there was mud under the pontoon so the damage was easily repairable.

Rod said calmly, "Our contract is complete, gentlemen. I expect the Stuart Sapphire within a week or you know the consequences. I'm sure we won't meet again."

He turned to go, then checked, "Oh, and Commander, have the bugs taken out of my house please."

Rod strode up the gangway and turned left into Wapping High Street. It felt pretty good to be carrying £20 million, and a clear getaway with it.

The P.M. had recovered his politician's air of self-importance, "Commissioner, provide me with an escort please. These must go to No.10 at once. I will call in the Crown Jewelers to make the necessary repairs. I will inform Her Majesty of their recovery and that they are intact. Meanwhile I'll call in the media and tell them the good news."

"Right, Sir", said the Commissioner, "I'll put forward Sergeant Morrison's name for the reward and publish Cooper's for promotion to Commander for his good work on the case."

They walked up to the police station with the Sergeant carrying the sackful of crowns and scepters. Creighton's face could be seen peering round the corner of his window, consumed with curiosity and annoyance at having been sidelined in his own Headquarters. He never would understand why.

Rod caught the first cab he came to and took it to the gym where Mike Corder worked. He was supervising some lads at boxing practice. His face brightened when he saw Rod, "Hallo, boss! Long time no see."

"Hallo, Mike, how have you been keeping?"

"Oh not so bad, struggling along." The elbows were out of his sweater and his shoes were army surplus.

Rod said, "Can you come outside for a while, Mike?"

"Sure, boss." They went and sat on a low wall.

Rod said, "I've got some news for you, Mike." Rod took the pardon with Mike's name on it and handed it to him. "This is a Royal Pardon, Mike. Don't lose it, it means you can't ever be nabbed for the job. And this is your bonus, five million."

Rod gave Mike the bank statement. He studied it for a moment, not taking it in at first, then tears began to run down his face. He sniffed and wiped his nose on his sleeve. He gripped Rod's arm and just said, "Thanks, boss."

"That's OK, Mike, couldn't have done it without you. Would you like to join us in Jersey in a week's time? We're going to collect some of the cash and have us a real party. Look, here's your ticket." Rod handed over the ticket and said, "We'll all be on the same plane."

"Sure, boss, wouldn't miss it." Gesturing over his shoulder with his thumb, Mike said with feeling, "And I can quit this bloody treadmill now as well!"

Rod found Bill Harding on his lunch break. His reactions were wonderment and total joy, "Bloody brilliant! What a genius old boot you are! Just wait till my old woman hears about this. Her eyes will go round like a ruddy cash register. Jersey? Yeah, you bet, we'll make some noise there, eh, boss!"

It was early evening when Rod drove up to Mac's pub. Mac knew at once to stop what he was doing and to walk outside. Outwardly his reactions to becoming a very rich man were quite calm, "Nice one, boss; knew you could do it; wouldn't have joined the outfit if I didn't think that. Now, about that beer you owe me." They both laughed and walked back towards the pub.

The Prime Minister was an expert media manipulator, as befitted his lifetime in politics. He had advised the Queen by telephone so she didn't hear the news from elsewhere. Now cameras and reporters jammed into Downing Street opposite No.10.

He oozed false modesty, "Yes, I played some part in it, but most credit must go to the Commissioner and his team, in particular Commander Cooper. They did all the spade work."

It was a brilliant touch. Attributing the 'spade work' to others made it seem like the 'brain work' had come from him.

"Who will get the reward? That will go to Sergeant Morrison of Thames Division, and could not be more deserved. It was only his great skill and bravery that enabled the jewels to be recovered in such dangerous circumstances. Yes, I will make a statement in Parliament later today. Her Majesty is naturally very pleased. No, no one has been apprehended yet, and we are still pursuing our inquiries, but the main thing is, as I'm sure you all agree, that we have recovered the Crown Jewels intact."

The papers splashed the headlines in the biggest type they had. Sergeant Morrison was suitably modest when interviewed on national television. He had been well briefed. But of course the media would see through his modesty. "Well, yes, it was a bit rough at times, I got trapped upside down by the legs, and my air was running out, but it was OK in the end." He looked suitably self-deprecating. "How did I know where to look? Well, my superiors had worked out that the jewels might be in a certain area, and I was just lucky to be the one who found them." The tabloids said it all:

'Hero Diver Risks Life For Jewels!'
'One Month Off Retirement Police Diver Gets Dream Bonus!'

The photos showed him outside his small house with proud wife and seven bemused youngsters arranged in age and size.

The P.M. kept his word. A small item in the press on the condition of the Crown Jewels made much of their miraculous survival after months in the River Thames. It was remarkable that so little damage had occurred. Only one minor stone was lost, a blue gem known as the Stuart Sapphire. No doubt a faulty setting had allowed it to be swept away. Further search for it would be fruitless. The tide was strong and the mud deep at that point.

Few at first thought the announcement significant, but the press picked it up and soon put two and two together. It was all too coincidental, they said, that the Stuart Sapphire should go missing at this time. The same time as the Act of Parliament was removed which allowed the Royal House of Stuart their chance to make a return and a legal claim upon the throne which was rightfully theirs.

Then someone working for the Royal Jewelers, who insisted on remaining anonymous, was paid a very large sum by one of the newspapers for revealing that the stone had in fact been recovered intact in the Imperial State Crown. It had later been removed and spirited away somewhere. No, he didn't know where, but the order for it's removal could only have come from the very highest quarters for it to have been carried out. The newspapers weren't stupid, this could only mean one thing, the Palace and No.10 colluding on it, but neither was talking. No one would admit to anything, despite enormous pressure from the media. So the supposed 'loss' of the Stuart Sapphire was widely disbelieved, and remained an unsolved mystery voiced by headlines like:

'Stuart Stone Goes Missing!'
'Secret Source Admits It Wasn't Lost!'

'Where Is The Stuart Sapphire?'
'Is The Stuart Sapphire Back Where It Belongs?
In The Hands Of The Stuart Royal House.'

'Return Of The Rightful Claimants?
Are The Stuarts On The Way Back?'

There was open discussion on TV of the likely return of the Stuarts. The Windsors had not acquitted themselves well in recent years. Their image had plummeted during the period of the tragic death of Princess Diana, when they were seen to be cold and uncaring. Now after the events surrounding the loss of the Crown Jewels, their ratings had never been so low. For the first time people began in large numbers to cold-shoulder royal functions. Invitations to garden parties at the Palace were returned; requests for minor members of the royal family to carry out openings began to dwindle; royal patronage in all it's forms from the Windsors was seen as inappropriate and unnecessary. This major change in public attitudes was a real turning point in British history.

The people as a whole were waking up to the realities of the nonsense which surrounded the whole apparatus of deference on which the Windsor myth had thrived, and which over the years they had so cleverly maintained. There arose what could only be called a common feeling of distaste, even of revulsion, for the Windsors and what they stood for, unaccountable privilege. And that they should either be swept away or at least allowed to decay and atrophy. The British, not revolutionary by nature, were content for the latter, and the process was well under way. Everyone understood, even if they didn't voice the feeling openly, that it was only a matter of time before the Windsors realized they had no rightful place in British society and stood down. This had become inevitable because all the ordinary people of the nation could see in their hearts where the right lay; it lay with the Stuart Royal House.

The phrase De Jure; By Right, From The Law, had done it's work.

At Rod's house a police van arrived and a team began to de-bug the place. They were doing this when an unmarked car containing four men drew up. The smallest of them, wearing glasses and carrying a small package, walked up to the house. Two burly guards, clearly with guns under their coats, accompanied him. On the doorstep Rod was invited to sign for the package.

He said, "I'd like to see the contents before I sign. The goons can stay outside."

The little man seemed hurt that Rod should be mistrustful. In the house the package was opened to reveal a small box containing cotton wool. Nestling in it was an egg-sized blue gemstone so bright it seemed to generate it's own light. Rod was no expert on gems but this certainly seemed genuine. No paste could do that. He checked it's size and shape against the pictures in the publications on the Crown Jewels. It was an exact match.

Rod said, "Thank you, I'll sign."

He was given a copy of the receipt and the man and his companions left in their car. The police team had done with their de-bugging and also left.

Rod took the box to his desk, and with the Stuart Sapphire glittering at him, typed a letter.

'Sir,
Please accept from your dutiful subjects in Britain the Stuart Sapphire. It has come from the Imperial State Crown and is genuine. It is rightfully yours. You will know what to do with it. It has been restored to it's rightful owners. It should pass to your family, who in turn will pass

it on. In time it will reside once more in a crown worn by a Stuart on the throne of Britain.

It should not be necessary for you to check the stone's authenticity, but should you choose to do so, please send a copy of this letter to the Prime Minister and the Commissioner of the Metropolitan Police in London. They will confirm the stone is genuine.

The gem cannot be returned. It has been bequeathed to the Royal House of Stuart in perpetuity.

My humble duty to you, Sir, and to your family.

Roderick Blood Jackson.
Captain, Royal Marines. (Retd).

Rod took a copy of the letter, then re-packaged the jewel carefully in it's box . He addressed it to Albert, Duke of Bavaria.

At the local post office he gave the package no special status. It went by normal post. Calculated risks were what Rod did.

He had never been a devout Catholic. To say he was lapsed would be to put it mildly. He had never been one for going to confession. But he felt an overwhelming need to tell someone, to share what he had done. At St. Thomas' Church in Woodbridge he knelt in the confessional.

He said quietly, "Father I have sinned", and made a brief outline of his actions and motives.

There was a pause from the priest, Father Peter, a long pause. Rod thought he heard sniffing followed by the priest blowing his nose.

Then in a voice choked with emotion the priest said quietly, "May the Holy Father and all the True Church give thanks. Go in peace my son. This was no sin, this was a blessing. Go in the grace of God."

Rod's sense of achievement was complete and he smiled as he rose to go. He knew his life had meant something. He felt uplifted, but quite unlike him he found tears running down his face.

The next day the plane ride to Jersey in the Channel Islands was fun. The four of them drank champagne and had some laughs, but on Rod's advice didn't overdo the drink as they needed their wits about them to handle the money side of things. In Jersey they got a taxi and headed for St. Helier and their bank. On the way Rod told the taxi driver to stop and gave him £10 to go for a short walk. Rod then talked to the others for a few minutes. They seemed agreed on what he said. The driver re-joined the car and they carried on into town.

In the bank Rod gave the four account numbers and waited while the clerk went through a door. Seconds later the manager appeared and smilingly ushered them into his office.

He shook hands all round, "Welcome, gentlemen, my name is Richards and I'm the manager here. It's a pleasure to be handling your accounts. My instructions are that you have been doing some work for the government of a highly confidential nature, and that I am to give you every assistance. If you would just like to give me the names and three copies of your signatures for our records, I'll have the details finalized shortly."

Rod replied, "Thank you, Mr. Richards, but we need to make a small change in the arrangements. You are holding £20 million in four accounts of £5 million each. We need to open a fifth account for a Mr. E. This will contain £4 million and each of us will contribute £1 million to it. There will be therefore now five accounts each of £4 million. I trust you can arrange this?"

"Certainly, Sir, that won't take long. I'll be back right away", and he bustled out of his office. True to his word he was back very quickly with the necessary papers. "Here you are, gentlemen, if you would fill in your names and provide the signatures?"

This they did, and Rod said, "The fifth account, that for Mr. E, the same terms will apply to that account as for ours. He will identify himself by producing this statement. That has your approval?"

"Certainly, Sir, that's quite in order."

Rod spoke with a grin towards the other three, "We'd like some immediate spending money for our stay here, ten thousand apiece ought to do it."

"Of course, Sir, that's no problem." Richards pressed a button and whispered instructions to an aide who entered and left, reappearing quickly with four neat bundles of £10,000. These Rod and the others took with satisfied smiles.

Richards said, "Where would you like your cards and cheque books delivered, Sir?"

"The Hotel Normandie", said Rod, naming the best hotel on the island.

"Certainly, Sir, the Normandie, and may I assume you would like me to arrange secure investments meanwhile for the five accounts?"

Rod replied, "Yes, by all means, and thank you for your help, you've been most kind."

Rod shook Richards by the hand. The Manager was all smiles. It was not every day he got the keeping and investment of £20 million. It was a good day's work for him, "It's been a real pleasure, Sir, and do contact me at any time for help with the accounts."

Rod picked up the bank statement made out for £4 million to Mr. E and asked for an envelope, Rod folded the statement into the envelope, and the four of them left the office to walk across the bank concourse to the exit. Rod was the last of the four. As the other three left, Rod passed a man sitting at a table with his back to them and reading a magazine. An open airline bag was on the table. As Rod went past he dropped the envelope into the bag, walked out and joined the others. They were all grinning, not knowing what to say.

165

Rod said it first, "Gentlemen, we are going to par-tee!" The emphasis on that last word left them in no doubt that they were going to have the hell-raising party of their lives. They walked off down the street laughing and yelling for a taxi.

Inside the bank, the man with the magazine put it down, zipped the flight bag and stood up. Putting the bag over his shoulder he strolled slowly out of the bank. From the back he looked familiar.

The magazine was still open. It showed a double-page spread of a brilliant red Ducati 996 motorcycle.

About the Author

Educated at University College, Oxford University, a contemporary of Bill Clinton and sharing the the same common room, the author remains undecided on the value of mentioning this. But service in the Royal Air Force and the British Army, and contacts with the Royal Navy, makes the author expertly qualified to write in convincing detail on the exciting action scenes in this fast paced thriller.

Inside knowledge too comes from contact with the British Royal family. The author lunched with the Queen and Prince Phillip in May 1999, and mentioned to the Prince that a way had been devised to steal the Crown Jewels. He seemed quite amused. Not only is it possible, this book shows how it can be done.

The results are certainly controversial, and are sure to stir a wide public reaction, but that's what makes the book such a good read.